MW00676884

A Georgia Sports History

To Angie

— Jeff Harris

A Georgia Sports History

An Overview of the Last Three Hundred Years

By

Jeffrey B. Harris

●YONAH PUBLISHING●

A Georgia Sports History
By Jeffrey B. Harris

Copyright © 2013 Yonah Publishing
Roswell, Georgia

All rights reserved. No part of this book may be reproduced or transmitted in any form by any means, electronic or mechanical, including photocopying and recording, or by any information storage and retrieval system, except as may be expressly permitted by the 1976 copyright Act or in writing from the publisher.

Dedicated to my wife, parents, students, and yomobo

"To get along with me, don't increase my tension."

-Ty Cobb

TABLE OF CONTENTS

1

— Introduction —

Seventeen year old Jimmy Wilson is on the mound in the bottom of the ninth inning. A bead of sweat drips down his cheek. He's trying to drown out the embarrassing cheers of his overly affectionate mother and focus on striking out Paul Goodson, the jerk who stole his girlfriend— and his reason for living. His buddies warming the bench make cat-calls to the batter as they don their rally caps. The wind up, the pitch, strike three! Other parents and bystanders drown out his mother's screams. All the players trot to the dugout and listen to the ranting of Coach Frank, while they eagerly await their post-game beverages (without sugar, no doubt). The team forms a circle for the coach's post-game prayer, as Jimmy revels in having saved the game, his dignity, —and perhaps won back his girl. It's June 5, 2011, Ball Ground, Georgia.

Eighteen-year-old Hyresse-Efy gets the deerskin ball in his stick, but he's about two hundred yards from the goal. He glances up at the batwing attached to his stick for luck and he sighs. The predominant concern on his mind is when the elders find out he was with his *hoktē* (woman) last night; they'll punish him for sure. Hyresse-Efy knows that abstinence is one of the rules of the game. But he finds it more appealing to do as he pleases than to follow the rules. He's a rebel, even by Creek standards. As he runs over one opponent and delivers a crushing blow to another, he doesn't have the luxury of looking back to see if his hit proved fatal. There are cheers from all sides, and spectators are in the thousands. He's run full speed for one hundred fifty yards and slings the stick as hard as he can. Goal!!!! One of the messengers heads over to the bushes, where the shaman is deep in prayer, to tell him the good news. It's June 5, 1711, Ball Ground, Georgia.

The settings of these two stories are the same, but they're three hundred years apart. It's not too often we hear of kids getting killed in little league, nor do they play to gain territory (except in cheesy

1980s movies like *One Crazy Summer*). The rules are of a different nature, but there are rules nonetheless. Each culture has its own superstitions, rituals, and traditions.

There is a long history and sporting heritage in the region we now call Georgia. Sports have evolved and taken on many forms, with each person liking the particulars of each game for different reasons. Games often bring people together, sometimes pull people apart, but always fill that void when you or your team wins!

What's Ahead?

The sporting tradition predates the written word. Starting with feats of strength through wrestling and racing, today's athletic competitions are world spectacles watched by millions. When you think of early sports, you may imagine gladiators fighting to the death in the Coliseum. Perhaps you think of ancient Egyptians racing around the pyramids. You may even envision naked men throwing javelins (whatever floats your boat). Sports have changed a great deal over thousands of years, but if you look closely you'll find a connection between the eras of the tomahawk and the "tomahawk chop."

This book presents a brief history of recreation, sports, teams, and the major figures that have made the headlines in the state of Georgia. First, we look at the pre-colonial period and see how the Native Americans spent their leisure time. (Heard of lacrosse?) Next we look at sports in Georgia from the colonial era to the Civil War. (The first person to gouge out the other person's eye is the winner!) Finally, we examine the formation and evolution of modern sports and the teams and athletes who have brought notoriety to this glorious state. Some of the rule changes, crazy stories, and record-breaking accomplishments of Georgia's stars will blow your pants off.

2

— Native Americans —

Many years ago, long before the Europeans set sail to call America their own, Native Americans were involved in a more ritualistic recreation than we're used to in our modern secular world. The contrast between the games of that world and ours is staggering, if not sometimes outrageous.

The Stickball Game

A Cherokee myth details an ancient game between the ground animals and the birds. As the story goes, a couple of tiny animals were treated unfairly by the deer, bear, and terrapin. They were mocked, laughed at, and basically told to get lost. Upset, the two decided on vengeance and hustled over to the side of their one-time enemy. As they told their plight to the leaders of the birds, the Great Hawk must have felt sympathetic, for he allowed them a place on his team of fowl and not a place in his belly.

Of course, there existed one problem: neither animal could fly. So they did some brainstorming and came up with a brilliant idea. The birds took the drum that set the rhythm during the pre-game entertainment and cut out the leather used for the drum head into the shapes of little wings, attached them to one of the mice-like creatures, and -ta-da- it's a bat! Uh oh, there's no more leather? What could they do for animal number two? One of the birds had the ingenious idea to stretch the skin of the second little fellow. So they pulled on his skin between his front and back legs for several minutes and -voila- it's a flying squirrel!

With the help of the flying squirrel and the bat, the birds won the game —bringing shame to the ground animals. It's sort of a David and Goliath-meets-Animal Planet -meets- *Extreme Makeover* kind of story. The lesson? If someone makes fun of the way you look, have some dramatic reconstructive surgery and challenge him (or her) to an epic battle.

The stickball game described in this Cherokee myth is what we call lacrosse. It's a lot different today than in the old days. I'd be willing to bet money the players of today don't do the following:

1. Practice abstinence from 'you know what' before games.
2. Allow a shaman to scratch twenty-eight lines onto each limb and be covered in blood.
3. Abstain from wonderful meals of frog, rabbit, or any baby animals.
4. Play naked.
5. Grease up their bodies to be as slippery as an eel.
6. Attach the cut-off wings of a bat to their sticks for good luck.
7. Conduct an elaborate ceremonial dance the night before a game.
8. Play with two sticks.
9. Play for several days in stormy weather.
10. Run more than a mile to the goal.

Despite all the rituals performed for one to four weeks before a game, the actual contest had very few rules. A Cherokee player used two sticks that looked similar to today's lacrosse sticks, but they were made of wood, and they used animal skin or hemp for the netting. The teams contained nine to twenty-two players per side and played on level ground with 100 to 400 yards between the goals (there's evidence suggesting that the playing field stretched over a mile in some cases). Evidence suggests that in some games there were well over a hundred players per team.

Spectators could be in the thousands, and some could be severely hurt during the games. Boundaries didn't mean much to these players. In *Travels in North America 1827-1828*, British naval officer Basil Hall published an account of a lacrosse game. He described how he jumped and held on-to a tree with all his might when the ball landed near him. But, he wrote, "a poor boy…had not time to imitate my example, and being overwhelmed by the multitude, was rolled over and over half-a-dozen times, in spite of his screams, which were lost in the clatter of sticks, and the yells and the shouts of the combatants…and were letting out the secret of their savage nature very fast."

The basic rules are listed below, but there were variations in each game and for each tribe:

1. Players line up in the middle of the playing field
2. The game begins with a throw in.
3. The deer-skin ball must first be picked up with the sticks
4. The player may drop his sticks and run with the ball
5. There was no "out of bounds"
6. After a score, the two captains face off, and it begins again
7. The first side to score twelve goals wins the game.

During the game, the coach –who was a shaman- stayed in the bushes reciting prayers in hopes of distracting the opposing team. Assistant coaches -called messengers- made trips from the field to the bushes to keep the shaman informed of the progress in the game.

According to Cherokee expert James Mooney:

> It is a very exciting game as well as a very rough one, and in its general features is a combination of baseball, football, and the old-fashioned shinny (hockey). Almost everything short of murder is allowable in the game, and both parties sometimes go into the contest with the deliberate purpose of crippling or otherwise disabling the best players on the opposing side. Serious accidents are common. In the last game which I witnessed one man was seized around the waist by a powerfully built adversary, raised up in the air and hurled down upon the ground with such force as to break his collar-bone. His friends pulled him out to one side and the game went on.

It was not uncommon for players to sustain severe injuries or even die. This was the result of a brutal game with few rules and no padding. Injuries were not necessarily a result of retribution, but Mooney noticed players who would start the game with the goal of taking out the opposing team's best players.

It is important to note that games were played between neighboring settlements and also between different tribes. The teams gambled with stakes that could range from small material possessions, all the wealth the team possessed, or a tribe's territory. Some believe the city of Ball Ground, Georgia, is so named because of a massive game played between the Cherokee and the Creeks, in which the former won the game and, consequently, the territory. Others believe the name of the city changed over the years from Battle Ground, named after the battle of Taliwa in 1755. Whatever the case, the ball game may have been more religious, political, and economic than recreational.

Gambling went hand in hand with the ball game and practically all the other games being played. According to anthropologist Charles Hudson, "after the ball had passed inspection, the players and spectators moved about holding up articles they wanted to wager on the outcome of the game. Sometimes the betting was so competitive that people would take off some of the clothing they were wearing in order to bet it." Sometimes players bet everything they owned. Native Americans from Georgia played all sorts of games of chance, but the focus of this book is on recreation that requires at least some dexterity.

Chunkey

Chunkey was THE game of the Mississippian Period (1000-1600). A myth explains that the game was created by Untsaiyi Brass, the god of gambling. The game was played by two men with poles. One rolled a stone disc slightly larger than a hockey puck down the field. Then the players threw their poles at the disc as it was coming to a stop. The player whose pole landed closest to the disc won a point.

Rules varied from tribe to tribe, but chunkey held equal importance among the tribes in the southeastern United States, including the Cherokee, the Creek, the Choctaw, and the Chickasaw. Just as modern cities have stadiums, each Indian town had a chunkey field. Chunkey discs were usually not the possessions of individuals, but the property of a particular clan.

Other Games

Ring and Pin- Ever heard of "cup and ball"? The ring is attached to the pin by some sort of cord. The ring is tossed into the air, and the player tries to catch the ring with the pin.

Shinny- The precursor to hockey... There isn't much evidence to suggest the southeastern tribes played this game.

Double ball- Two balls were attached by a cord and flung with a stick. Sorry fellas, double ball remained exclusively a women's game.

Marbles- More like bocce-golf- It was played with stones the size of billiards balls and typically took place on a five-hole course

Archery- The good ol' bow and arrow- Before serious fire power, it was the way to hunt. Native Americans began using the bow and arrow in the Woodland period, sometime before the year 1000. Considering this was the main way to obtain their food, the natives held shooting matches that tested accuracy.

3

— Colonial Days to the Civil War —

"Corn shuckin's, house raisin's, quiltin's, pea thrashin's, singin's, log rollin's, candy pullin's."
-Eliot Wigginton

At the founding of colonial Georgia, when the trustees made all the rules, settlers faced four restrictions: the amount of land one could own (*Wait, is this communist Russia?*), no slaves (*Wow, all right Georgia!*), no rum (*I'm out!*), and no Catholics (*No hell!*). James Oglethorpe, the colony's founder, believed the land limits would create a society of yeoman farmers who wouldn't be spaced too far away to withstand the Spanish, if they were to attack.

Eventually, the trustees turned over the colony to the British crown, making it a royal colony and the rules faded away.

So the planters appropriated more land and purchased hundreds of slaves to work their plantation. With time for leisurely activities, they led lives comparable to England's landed gentry. As soon as slaves entered the picture, author Elliott Gorn writes, "black...slavery made it difficult for whites to venerate work, easy for them to idealize play." Those who lived this upper-class life hunted, attended horse races, dueled, and watched cock-fights.

During the day, the planters and their male relatives enjoyed fox hunts, and at night slaves usually joined in. Night-time hunts included chasing raccoons and possums. Other activities included, dice games and horse races, in which "the jockeys and many of the spectators" were black according to historian Urlich Phillips.

For the most part, the slaves' recreation was similar to that of the yeoman farmers: it revolved around work.

Slave Recreation

In antebellum Georgia, slaves were supposed to have a day of rest on Sunday. Although this didn't happen on every plantation, it allowed some slaves an opportunity for entertainment. While many spare-time activities, like corn-shucking, revolved around work, some recreation glimpsed vestiges of African culture.

Just as the banjo has its roots in Africa, so did some sports played by the few slaves who had free time. These included foot races, wrestling, and jumping contests, which were rites of passage in the African homeland. As time went on, many African cultural elements disappeared, replaced by pastimes of the American cultural stew.

Hunting and fishing were regular activities and generally done at night. Former slave John Van Hook recalled in 1938, that he "hunted rabbits, squirrels, coons, all kinds of birds, and 'specially fond of going after wild turkeys. Another great sport was hunting deer in the nearby mountains." Former slave William Hutson remembered "there was a creek not far away and they was good fishing in the stream and squirrels in the trees...lot of fun to catch them fishes."

Cornshuckings were the typical form of amusement revolving around the work that needed to be done. Van Hook remembered:

> Great excitement was expressed whenever a man found a red ear of corn, for that counted 20 points, a speckled ear was 10 points and blue ear 5 points, toward a special extra big swig of liquor whenever a person had as many as 100 points...after the work...they played ball, tussled, ran races, and did anything they knew how to amuse themselves.

As boxing and wrestling made their way to the plantation, so did town ball. This precursor to baseball was played all over the South, though it most likely was invented in New England. There is much evidence in slave narratives that this game was not played by blacks alone, but was an integrated activity. The players used cotton wrapped in rags and any sturdy branch as a bat. Over time, town-ball led to America's national pastime...baseball.

Many slave narratives from the *Freedom Writers Project* in the 1930s told of activities that included town-ball, marbles, football, boxing, and horseracing. In one narrative, Theodore Fontaine Stewart recalled how his father was put on a horse to race another slave and won so decisively that his owner removed him from the field and made him work the stable instead. Apparently, it wasn't often that slaves rode in horse races, but over time slaves and free blacks became jockeys in some of the biggest races in America.

In addition to slaves and the planter class, yeoman farmers represented the majority of the population in Georgia before the Civil War. Many of these families lacked slaves and lived by the sweat of their brow. So they had little time for goofing around. Since there were time constraints in the laborious day, they often combined work and play. Just as many people today hunt and fish for recreation, so did early inhabitants nearly 300 years ago. But these fun pastimes were often required to put food on the table.

Other forms of recreation on the farm correlated with the fall harvest. Whether it was log rolling, corn shucking, fodder pulling, barn raising, or hog killing, young men found competition and joy in activities others might find tedious. According to author Richard Kraus, other games in the Southern colonies included "bear-baiting, bull-baiting, bowling, cards, quoits (horseshoes), dice, football, ninepins, and tennis."

In the South, people were so spread out because of the agrarian lifestyle that recreation was often individual or in small groups. There is evidence that in cities there were more team games like cricket, but in the country, games were mostly individual and related to work, or sometimes survival. For example, James Oglethorpe, Georgia's founder, organized shooting contests. Those who were most accurate won five or ten shillings. But the main purpose of these contests concerned the issue of Spain being next door to Georgia, in Florida. So it was best to have settlers who can handle firearms.

Popular sports of today existed at this point; tennis and golf were common in England. Surely, a few settlers in Georgia were playing their own versions of England's games of high society. Many Englishmen headed to the Georgia colony, where the planter class replicated many aspects of English society. There's mention of cricket in early Georgia documents, but one activity of the early inhabitants of Georgia brought over from merry ole London dealt with honor...

Dueling

Dueling was a method of "obtaining satisfaction" and protecting honor. It declined after the American Revolution, but was "full speed ahead" at Georgia's infancy. There were many ways to duel: taking turns shooting at your opponent, using swords, or even throwing bowie knives. Whatever the method, the end result was either a flesh wound or a new home with the worms.

"Your daddy's a no good, stinkin' rascal!" Has anyone talked some trash about a member of your family? What if you decided to demand satisfaction and challenge the SOB to a duel? You shoot him, he dies, everything's back to normal. You return to your job, play with your kids, or watch your favorite episode of *Gimme a Break*. Sound ridiculous? This is exactly what happened in 1828 with Attorney General George Crawford (*he was a big fan of Nell Carter*). Apparently, Congressman Thomas Burnside published some unflattering remarks about Crawford's father (*oh no he didn't!*). Crawford challenged Burnside to a duel. He accepted, as everyone did unless he was a total wuss. After each man missed a few times, Crawford finally hit his target and Burnside died almost instantly. Here's the twist: Burnside never wrote anything about Crawford's father. A woman had written it, but remained anonymous, and Burnside defended the article for her.

Another famous duel in Georgia's history deals with Button Gwinnett and Lachlan McIntosh. (Counties were named for each man and Button was a signer of the Declaration of Independence.) Who's gonna win? *Well, obviously a guy named "Button" isn't going to win a duel.* This duel took place in the midst of the American Revolution. Gwinnett was not happy with his place in executive order and made poor choices in military strategy. McIntosh, a general, called Gwinnett a 'scoundrel' before the Georgia assembly. This was like being called the queen mother of dirty words in those days. Gwinnett wrote him a challenge to meet before dawn. The men faced each other and fired at the same time. Each was hit in the thigh. McIntosh asked if he had "gained satisfaction" or if he'd like another go at it. Mr. Buttons said he felt vindicated, then died twelve days later from his wound.

Gouging

For people living in the frontier or backcountry, sports took on a much different meaning. These people weren't upper-class gentry, and any status they gained was usually acquired through violence. Life in the backcountry was, as famously expressed by Thomas Hobbes in *Leviathan,* "solitary, poor, nasty, brutish, and short."

Imagine mixed martial arts with no rules. Now picture Biff Tannen calling Marty McFly a chicken. Finally, envision Marty biting off Biff's nose and gouging his eye out, with Marty's pseudo-incestuous mother cheering him on. Like dueling, this fight dealt with defending one's honor, but with a type of boxing called gouging or rough-and-tumble fighting. The object of the fight: gouge out the other guy's eyeball.

In an article published in *American Historical Review,* Elliott Gorn quoted what one out-of-place circuit court judge said about what he saw in the backcountry: "Before God, gentlemen…, I never saw such a thing before in the world. There is a plaintiff with an eye out! A juror with an eye out! And two witnesses with an eye out!" Georgia legally banned this "sport" in the mid-eighteenth century. A person could go to jail for several years for gouging out someone's eyeball. But in all probability gouging continued until the revolver became a common possession, making it easier to settle disputes.

As Gorn noted, "men drink together, tongues loosen, a simmering old rivalry begins to boil; insult is given, offense taken, ritual boasts commence; the fight begins, mettle is tested, blood redeems honor, and equilibrium is restored."

Because of rough-and-tumble fighting, many an "honorable" man was missing an eye, had a ripped-off ear, or a bitten-off nose.

Many accounts of rough-and-tumble fighting were written by travelers unaccustomed to this type of honor defending. In *Stranger in America,* first published in 1807, Charles William Janson wrote:

> We found the combatants' fast clinched by the hair, and their thumbs endeavoring to force a passage into each other's eyes; while several of the bystanders were betting upon the first eye to be turned out of its socket. For some time the combatants avoided the *thumb stroke* with dexterity. At length they fell to

the ground, and in an instant the uppermost sprung up with his antagonist's eye in his hand!

The savage crowd applauded, while, sick with horror, we galloped away from the infernal scene. The name of the sufferer was John Butler, a Carolinian, who, it seems, had been dared to the combat by a Georgian; and the first eye was for the honor of the state to which they respectively belonged. (*Go Georgia!*)

In some instances, the end result may have been worse than the loss of an eye, ear, or nose. Think about it... (When was the protective cup invented?)

Cudgeling

Remember when you were a kid and your mom would take you to the cudgeling match every Saturday morning and sometimes you'd forget the grip tape for your 'beating' club? *Come again?* No, you don't remember, because we don't live in a society where we would beat each other's brains in with clubs. *We don't?*

The sport has its roots in the Middle Ages and, in the 1904 Olympic Games, became an event called 'singlestick'. For many men, it was a training tactic for fencing, but many a ruffian considered it a sport on its own. The winner was the person who drew first blood on their opponent's head. These matches were common among the Scotch-Irish immigrants in the backcountry, where religious rules against violent endeavors could not apply.

President Theodore Roosevelt was known to be a spectator and a participant at cudgeling matches. Roosevelt once said, "Speak softly but carry a big stick." Perhaps he was talking about cudgeling? In a letter to James Garfield Roosevelt wrote, "Late in the afternoon I played at single stick with General Wood (coached Georgia Tech) and Mr. Ferguson. We have to try to hit as light as possible, but sometimes we hit hard, and today I have a bump over one eye and a swollen wrist."

In the brutal matches in the Georgia backcountry, brain damage was much more likely.

Bearbaiting and Bullbaiting

You may be wondering if a "sport" could be more violent than gouging or cudgeling. The answer is yes, although in this case the violence involves animals, not humans. Bearbaiting and bullbaiting involved a pack of pit dogs against a lone bear or bull. The promoters of these events may have blown pepper into the bull's nose to make it enraged, and then released several dogs on the bull, possibly up to twenty. Baiting was popular in England but started to wane by the eighteenth century and was banned in 1835. In England, breeders developed dogs that would dominate in the ring; these are the ancestors of bulldogs and pit bulls. Today's bulldogs are much smaller than their ancestors, leaving just a glimpse of the ferociousness that once existed.

Bearbaiting was less popular, but only because of the difficulty in obtaining a bear. But the spectacle was another wholesome activity in the Southern backcountry. The bear had a collar around its neck that was tied to a post in the ground. Some bears had been declawed and had their teeth removed so that the dogs would have a better chance at winning. Although seen as cruel, royalty like King Henry VIII and Queen Elizabeth I were fans of this entertainment, and it still happens today in countries like Pakistan. Unfortunately, it has also been known to happen in rural areas of South Carolina.

The baiting spectacles began to fall out of favor in the early to mid-nineteenth century. It would be safe to say most people are not proponents of animal cruelty and don't believe animals should be used in such a manner. On the other hand, cruelty to animals for sport still exists. Just ask Michael Vick... *Didn't he run an illegal dog fighting operation?* Yes.

Cockfighting

With its beginnings in the Old World, cockfighting found its way over to Europe during the Middle Ages and then to the New World with the Spanish and the English. Georgia outlawed cockfights in 1775, but since when have laws ever stopped anything...?

Usually, cockfighting was done outside of a tavern, where patrons wagered on the bird of their choice. Breeding was specialized and the roosters that fought were equal in size, for the most part. *Like the weight system in boxing? Good job, little buddy.* Fights usually lasted until one of the birds became incapacitated or wound up dead.

Although people from all backgrounds participated in cockfights on one level or another, there was a Southern faux pas being committed. As the South became more evangelical, cockfighting went against the moral code imposed by ministers and soft-hearted women. As Ted Ownby writes, it was "a scene of wild-eyed, half-crazed, shouting men, watching two angry cocks slicing at each other's throats, pecking at each other's eyes, and battling to a possibly bloody death." *Now, what's so immoral about that...?*

It could also be said that cockfighting was symbolic of Southerners in general. Cockfights in the South differed from this the North. In the North, the gaffs, or blades, that were attached to the heel of the bird were much shorter than in the South. The short gaffs allowed the fight to last longer, and it was based more on skill and finesse. In the South it was about long gaffs and power. Needless to say, the Southern cockfights were quick and gory.

Horse Racing

The number one spectator sport goes great with a mint julep, or is it the other way around? *He's cut off, bar- keep!* Lacking the thoroughbreds the old world was racing, colonists were racing smaller horses lacking superior endurance. The majority of the horses used were Chickasaws, named after the southern Indian tribe that brought them up from Spanish Florida.

Horses raced on dirt tracks or roads for a quarter mile. Early on, the owners themselves rode their horses and it would often times get pretty rough. The riders sometimes tried to bump or trip an opponent's horse ...anything to win. Quarter racing was typically a pastime of the planter class, but eventually people of all social classes gathered to watch and make side wagers. In one instance, a tailor entered his horse in a race for the prize of 2000 pounds of tobacco. The county court fined him 200 pounds of tobacco, stating that horseracing was a sport for "gentlemen".

According to Hunt Boulware of Western Carolina University, "Race courses throughout the low country transcended the realm of mere sporting arenas and evolved into venues where personal fortunes were squandered and secured, political futures and family connections strengthened, and social and business transactions of every manner conducted, and amusements of all kinds indulged."

As fairs moved into rural settings and brought with them horse racing on a larger scale, evangelicals protested the sport's sinful nature. It was not necessarily the races themselves that went against the moral code, but the elements that coincided with the sport, gambling and drinking, which led to fighting and fornicating.

Owning a race horse was a sign of wealth and raised ones social status. As time passed, racing grew in popularity and changed. Races held on oval tracks specifically for spectators became more about gambling than about honor or pastime. After the colonial period, most jockeys were slaves and spectators were people of all classes and races.

Gander Pulling

Here's the setting:

A goose is tied up by its feet, hanging from a pole. A man on horseback must ride at full speed to try and grab the goose's head, and then pull it off. Oh yeah, it's alive and greased up for added difficulty. Milledgeville's *Union Recorder* newspaper from Valentine's Day 1888 reported:

> The...scene was C.B. Pelton riding a mule. When he passed the gander he caught him by the neck with both hands, but he could not pull his head off. He hung on for dear life. His mule left him, and he found himself sitting on the ground. I think everybody laughed until they cried.

For the most part, if one pulled the head off, the reward was a goose to cook for dinner. This varied from town to town, with betting a common occurrence. Gander pulling fell out of favor by the end of the nineteenth century. Writings of the late 1800s show that people looked down upon this horrible pastime. The *Columbus Enquirer-Sun* from January 3, 1888, reported about the goose that "the poor thing soon learned its enemies, and would quack and quail at the approach of the rider. This was enjoyable to the hard-hearted, but shocking to the more tender. It is hoped they will seek a sport next time more suited to civilization."

Hunting

Well before Georgia's Trustee period (1732-1752), hunting was a wee bit different. Native Americans sought more than just deer; they hunted mammoth and giant ground sloths, and all the time had to look out for the American lion, bulldog bear, and perhaps the dire wolf. After the mega fauna became extinct, the animals of Georgia were similar to what we have today, but most people don't realize that even modern animals have been overhunted to near extinction. The white-tailed deer, for example, was completely wiped out in Georgia around the turn of the twentieth century; it had to be reintroduced to the region.

Hunting was a necessary endeavor to obtain extra food for the farmers. Not only did it provide more meat, it helped the men gain knowledge of the backcountry terrain which came in handy during times of war. The prey ranged from squirrel, rabbits, possums, and raccoons to deer, elk, bear, and...human. *"You serious Clark?"* No.

Hunting differed a bit for the planter class, which went out on horseback with many slaves. The slaves would bring makeshift lanterns to en-trance the deer (think of modern-day car headlights). There was a healthy supply of deer in those days, and it was common for hunters to start on the trail of one and end up taking down another.

Fox hunting was popular among the planter class and represented the English cultural heritage among Georgians with land, money, and slaves. Even before the founding of Georgia, fox hunts were common in Virginia and can later be read about in the diaries of George Washington. Clubs developed over time with the earliest one, called the Piedmont Foxhounds, started in 1840; it still exists today.

Fox hunting involves hunters on horseback, for the most part, and a pack of foxhounds. They would find a fox trail and follow it until they found the den. The hunters wore traditional clothing with the black hat and red jacket. The reason for the red jackets is most likely to stand out just as today's hunters wear orange...

Ninepins/Skittles/Tenpins

Ninepins, or skittles, is the precursor to bowling. Its origins go back to ancient Egypt. It eventually made its way to fourth century Germany. Skittles involved throwing a wooden ball from a distance and attempting to knock down pins. This went on for a certain number of rounds, keeping track of the number of pins each player knocked down. Ninepins was apparently a bit different, in that the first player to knock down all the pins won.

As ninepins and skittles made their way to North America, they evolved into tenpins. Legend has it that gambling started to become a problem with ninepin games, and the local religious folk didn't take too kindly to this devilish play. Laws were created to ban ninepins, so the clever players decided to add one more pin and call it tenpins, so players weren't breaking any laws.

Quoits

Quoits is similar to horseshoes, except that, instead of a horseshoe, a ring about six inches in diameter is thrown on-to a spike. The game was popular among youth, and older members of high society indulged as well. There were quoits clubs whose members included lawyers, doctors, and judges. US Chief Justice John Marshall was supposedly a wizard at quoits.

Cricket

Cricket is a bat and ball game that developed in England in the sixteenth century. It made its way to America and was first mentioned in writing in the early 1700s. William Stephens, a planter living in Georgia wrote that the townsmen participated in a cricket match in the town square in 1737. Popular until the American Revolution, cricket was later thrown back across the ocean, with all the other British hobbies.

Of course, it wasn't that simple, but the games of cricket and baseball reflect the cultures of the two peoples. The 1859 *New York Herald* stated that cricket was "too slow, intricate and plodding a game for our go ahead people." Cricket revolves around the wickets (knocking them down means 'you're out!'), the bowler, the wicket-keeper, and the batman. The fielding positions are numerous and are chosen based on the captain's strategy. Some of the positions include deep fine leg, second slip, gully, silly point, short mid-wicket, tiddly bonker, square leg, long off, and extra cover. One of those was made up, but which one…?

4

— Baseball —

Way Back When...

21

Do you remember playing '21' growing up as a kid? And yes, I'm talking about basketball. *Why is he talking about basketball in the baseball chapter?* I'll tell you why. Imagine instead of playing '21' with a buddy on your driveway, you're on a baseball field competing with another team. This is the way it worked according to the 1845 Knickerbocker rules. By today's standards, the first team to reach 21 runs could possibly take a day and a half.

Softball

Yeah I said it. The first games of baseball were pitched underhand. *Is that Geena Davis on the mound?* No, it's not.

Bounce Out

It's a short fly ball to left field. Smith is running in and decides not to put in that extra effort to dive. OH NO! He caught it on the hop. His lack of bravado didn't matter in the least bit because the batter is out. That's right, in the good ol' days, whether it's caught on the fly or one hop...YOUR OUT!

He's Up Again?

Prior to 1854, the batting order was that of legend. Freddy Homerunsky batted clean-up in the first inning. Now he's batting cleanup in the second inning. Wait, it's the third inning and he's batting clean-up —again. Imagine Hank Aaron getting close to 10 at-bats a game— *Jeez, he would've had like 7000 homeruns.* No.

No Called Strikes

"No sir, I did not care for that pitch, hurl it again...and wait for me to adjust my monocle." The called strike wasn't introduced until 1858.

Take Your Base

In 1876, the rule was set for poor pitching. If a 'hurler' threw nine balls that were nearly impossible to hit, then the 'striker' would take his base. This gradually decreased one ball at a time until the National League settled on four in 1889.

Call Your Pitch

"If you wouldn't mind, could you hurl me a highball?" Batters in the 1870s could ask the pitcher for a high pitch or a low pitch. This was truly a batter's game.

Hey, Was That Out?

"Pardon me, sir?" says the umpire, *"I was watching the buxom blonde over by the beer stand and I just happened to miss that hit over by the third base line —Help a guy out, will ya?"* An umpire could ask someone in the stands their opinion on whether the play was fair. All spectators were men of honor who would never be biased —*Cough.*

No Gloves, Wussy

Not really a rule, but players in the old days didn't wear gloves. When gloves were first worn they were closer to batting gloves with the tips cut off than to the gigantic gloves of today. Some of the earliest glove-wearers had them painted a flesh color, so as not to cause a scene and be called a 'nancy'.

Wrong Way, Timmy!

Some of the earliest known rules required that the base runner round the bases in a counter clockwise fashion. They should have this happen in the majors on Opposite Day. Seriously, there is actually an Opposite Day, January 25th.

Peg 'em!

Remember playing wiffle ball in the back yard and playing with pegs? Remember pegging your neighbor when he was actually close enough to tag and he freaked out and grabbed the closest bat (which was a wooden one) and proceeded to throw it at you from ten feet away and give you a concussion? No, you don't remember? Just me? —Anyway, the earliest accounts of baseball allowed pegging the base runner...

The 250 Foot Home Run

Originally, the home run meant that a batter was able to round all the bases. Eventually, the rule about hitting the ball over the fence developed. In 1925, the minimum distance for a home run was set at 250 feet.

History

The name Abner Doubleday was created to put a face to a fabricated story on the origins of baseball. In 1907, a committee responsible for finding the true origins of the game came back with the Doubleday story. But historians have found no credible evidence to suggest he was the first to come up with the game of baseball.

Alexander Cartwright is considered to be the true father of baseball. He started a club called the New York Knickerbocker Base Ball Club and these are the rules the club played by:

1. Members must strictly observe the time agreed upon for exercise, and be punctual in their attendance.

2. When assembled for exercise, the President, or in his absence, the Vice-President, shall appoint an umpire, who shall keep the game in a book provided for that purpose, and note all violations of the By-Laws and Rules during the time of exercise.

3. The presiding officer shall designate two members as Captains, who shall retire and make the match to be played, observing at the same time that the players opposite to each other should be as nearly equal as possible, the choice of sides to be then tossed for, and the first in hand to be decided in like manner.

4. The bases shall be from "home" to second base, forty-two paces; from first to third base, forty-two paces, equidistant.

5. No stump match shall be played on a regular day of exercise.

6. If there should not be a sufficient number of members of the Club present at the time agreed upon to commence exercise, gentlemen not members may be chosen in to make up the

match, which shall not be broken up to take in members that may afterwards appear; but in all cases, members shall have the preference, when present, at the making of a match.

7. If members appear after the game is commenced, they may be chosen in if mutually agreed upon.

8. The game to consist of twenty-one counts, or aces; but at the conclusion an equal number of hands must be played.

9. The ball must be pitched, not thrown, for the bat.

10. A ball knocked out of the field, or outside the range of first or third base, is foul.

11. Three balls being struck at and missed and the last one caught, is a hand out; if not caught is considered fair, and the striker bound to run.

12. If a ball be struck, or tipped, and caught, either flying or on the first bound, it is a hand out.

13. A player running the bases shall be out, if the ball is in the hands of an adversary on the base, or the runner is touched with it before he makes his base; it being understood, however, that in no instance is a ball to be thrown at him.

14. A player running who shall prevent an adversary from catching or getting the ball before making his base, is a hand out.

15. Three hands out, all out.

16. Players must take their strike in regular turn.

17. All disputes and differences relative to the game, to be decided by the Umpire, from which there is no appeal.

18. No ace or base can be made on a foul strike.

19. A runner cannot be put out in making one base, when a balk is made by the pitcher.

20. But one base allowed when a ball bounds out of the field when struck.

The game of baseball could be considering a northern city phenomenon, but it would eventually make its way to the south. The Civil War brought two distinct cultures together and many Southerners, for the first time became aware of a game that had its beginnings a north of the Mason-Dixon Line. Sure, early games like rounders and, town ball were played in Dixie, so obviously baseball made its way to several southern towns. As Bell Irvin Wiley restates from a Confederate soldier's journal in *The Life of Johnny Reb*, "When leisure and weather permitted, soldiers turned out in large numbers for baseball. Captain James Hall of the Twenty-fourth Alabama Regiment observed that his men, while Joe Johnston was waiting at Dalton to see what Sherman was going to do, played baseball 'just like school boys.'"

Professional Baseball

May 12, 1866, was the first day of professional baseball in Atlanta *(that damn Sherman ain't gonna keep us down!)*. Tom Burnett started the Atlanta Baseball Club and it took on Robert Dohme's Gate City Nine. Gate City was one of Atlanta's many nicknames, along with Hotlanta, ATL, Dogwood City, the Big Peach, and the Chicken's Nipple. The 'hurlers' would leisurely toss the ball assuring those in the stands that this would be one heck of a high-scoring game. The Gate City Nine won the game 127-29.

It seems that baseball in Atlanta faded from the sporting scene for a bit. *The Daily Atlanta Intelligencer* published a brief story on the disappearance of baseball on June 9, 1870:

> What has become of the lovers of baseball? Are there no clubs? Can't we get up a match game between the club here, (if there is one,) and the Macon club, or any other club from any other...town? Or is it the truth that baseball lies in its grave...

After several years and a variety of teams rising and falling, the first professional league in the South emerged. The Southern League started in 1885, with Henry Grady acting as the president. Grady ran the league out of his office at the *Atlanta Constitution*, while also promoting the city to northern investors. *Busy guy.* There were several teams throughout Georgia, including Columbus (Stars), Atlanta (Atlantas), Augusta (Browns), and Macon. After about seven years of ups and downs and no league play for a couple of years, the Southern League rose again in 1892. Atlanta went through a couple more team names over the next few years, like the Firecrackers and the Windjammers.

Other cities throughout Georgia had teams in the minor leagues as well. Columbus started with the Stars, but held other names like the River Snipes (1896, 1907), Babies (1897), Foxes (1909-1932), Turfs (1931-1932), Red Birds and Cardinals (1936-1955), Confederate Yankees (1964-1966) *What?*, Astros (1970-1988), Mudcats (1989-1990), Indians (1991), Red Stixx (1992-2002), and Catfish (2003-2008).

Macon held names like the Hornets, Highlanders, Brigands, Peaches, Tigers, Pirates, Braves, and, most recently, Music. Augusta had the Browns, Electricians, Tourists, Georgians, Tigers, Wolves, Rams, Yankees, and since 1994, the GreenJackets (Masters). Savannah's nicknames included Dixies, Oglethorpe, Pathfinders, Indians, Colts, A's, Redlegs, Senators, Braves, Cardinals, and, the latest, Sand Gnats.

Although there have been teams in cities like Albany, Thomasville, Waycross and about three dozen more, it's the nicknames that draw considerable attention. Names like Millionaires, Frogs, Babies, Confederate Yankees, Nuts, Sea Cows, Pallbearers, Bees, Peaches, and to say again, Pallbearers! Good stuff.

Also, some of the Major League's best players got their start, or ended their careers in some of these ball clubs. Pete Rose was a Macon Peach in 1962 (batted .330), before his record-breaking MLB career with the Reds and the Phillies. Ty Cobb played for the Augusta Tourists in 1904, and the infamous North Carolinian, "Shoeless" Joe Jackson, played for Americus and the Waycross Coast Liners a few years after the notorious Black Sox Scandal.

While teams in Georgia consisted of some big names, there were also some original Southern nicknames. Nicknames seemed to be a sign of the times and while there were a half dozen "Pugs", there were just as many "Docs" (something tells me they didn't go to medical school). Some other nicknames of former Georgia ball players included Jocko, Hack, Dixie, Wheezer, Moose, Cowboy, Bobo, Coot, Chick, Smokey, Skeeter, Choo-Choo, and Nig. Nig was often used as a nickname for white people with dark complexions, and it thankfully fell out of favor after integration. *I would hope so!*

Georgia's minor-league teams have fared well in recent years. The Savannah Sand Gnats won the league title in 1993, 1994, and 1996. The Augusta GreenJackets won league titles in 1989, 1995, 1999, and 2008. The Gwinnett Braves (formerly the Richmond Braves and the Atlanta Crackers before that) had five league titles when they were in Richmond.

Atlanta Crackers

What's a Cracker? Well, there is no definitive answer to this question. It's most common usage has been to describe a poor white farmer. It has also been used to describe the plantation overseer, who would crack the whip over the slaves. These seem to be a bit too pejorative to be a team's nickname, especially when one considers that the Atlanta Black Crackers were descendants of slaves. Some have suggested that the name comes from the crack of the bat when a player gets a hit. Still others, as suggested by Atlanta Cracker expert Tim Darnell, think it could be an abbreviated name of the 1892 Atlanta Firecrackers.

The Atlanta Crackers made their 1896 debut in an unfinished season, when they dropped out after 72 games. Making headway and moving to Ponce de Leon Park in 1907, the Crackers won the pennant. The Georgia Railway and Electric claimed total ownership and the president was John Heisman (namesake of the Heisman Trophy). About four pennants later, in 1923, a fire burned down Ponce de Leon Park, leaving Rell Jackson Spiller to spend $250,000 on a baseball park masterpiece. The most unique part of the new "Spiller" park was the giant magnolia tree about 450 feet out in center field.

Another aspect of early Cracker baseball was 'playing the ponies.' Gambling took place in the outfield bleachers, and wagers were more than just a bet on the final score of the game. The spectators bet on what would happen for practically every pitch. When gambling was finally banned, it still thrived under the radar.

One promising fact about the Crackers team was that the price tag constantly changed and, at least in the beginning, in an upward direction. In 1905, Wally Joyner (later mayor of Atlanta) purchased the team for $20,000. In 1915, city councilman Frank Reynolds and J. W. Goldsmith Jr. bought the team for $37,000. In 1933, Coca-Cola bought the Crackers. After several years under Coke's control, Earl "Mr. Atlanta Baseball" Mann became owner in 1949, when he purchased the team for around $450,000.

In the mid-1950s, the club's value scaled down to several hundred thousand dollars, and was losing value quickly. Mann surrendered control to the Southern Association in the late fifties after profit losses. With the addition of television to people's living rooms, couch-potatoism began to take control of the Atlanta public, hurting and -perhaps- causing the demise of the Crackers. Oh yeah, the coming of the Braves may have played a part too…

The Black Crackers

The Crackers hosted some exhibition games with the Brooklyn Dodgers in 1949. The Grand Dragon of the Ku Klux Klan supposedly called the organization to demand that the game be cancelled due to African-Americans on the team, like Jackie Robinson and Roy Campanella. The threats were ignored, and for the first time in the history of professional sports, blacks and whites played ball together in Atlanta. This marked the end of the Negro Leagues and the beginning of integration.

African American baseball had been organized at Atlanta colleges, like Clark University and Atlanta University, by the 1890s. A few years earlier, the League of Colored Baseball Players had its start. On the professional side was Atlanta's first African American pro team, the Deppens. After they faded from the light, a new team emerged called the Atlanta Cubs, and in 1919 the Cubs changed their name to the Black Crackers. They would join the Negro Southern League in 1920.

It was not champagne and caviar for the Black Crackers, but it definitely beat share-cropping. The financial situation associated with the league was anything but stable. Two balls were used per game, which brought the game to a standstill when someone hit a homerun and you had to go find the ball. They could play at Ponce de Leon Park, but only if the Crackers were on the road. Otherwise, they played at one of the Atlanta universities, like Morehouse or Clark.

Also, practically everything that the club used (equipment, uniforms, etc.) was donated by the Atlanta Crackers.

It was also difficult for the players to find a place to stay when away from home. While the Black Crackers were on the road, the players would either pile into a few hotel rooms or stay in someone's house for a few bucks. The pay could range from fifty cents to a dollar per game, depending on the overhead and turnout for each game.

Some of the players and coaches who became fixtures of the Atlanta Black Crackers had colorful nicknames. "Chin" Evans, "Red" Moore, "Pee Wee" Butts, "Black Rider" Brown, "Pig" or "Pea" Greene, "Bubbles" Brown, "Jew Baby" Bennette, "Fireball" Colzie, "Bang" Long, "Soup" Reeves, "Babe" Davis, "Flit" Holliday, "Bozo" Jackson, "Gabby" Kemp, and "Fluke" Mitchell were just some of the players' nicknames.

The Black Crackers eventually moved to Indiana and became the Indianapolis ABCs in the newly formed Negro American League. This was short lived, and they quickly moved back to Atlanta until the league disbanded in 1952. Some of the best baseball players in the world were part of the Negro League, but most of their statistics were carelessly cast aside, so it's difficult to find out where they stand against some of the Major League's best.

Atlanta Braves

As many know, the Braves came to Atlanta from Milwaukee in 1966, but their story goes back a bit further than that. The Braves franchise made its start in 1876, making it the longest professional sports franchise in the history of America. The team went from the Boston Red Stockings to the Beaneaters, the Doves, the Rustlers, and finally rested on the Braves in 1912. Most people know the Braves' immortals, like Hank Aaron, Warren Spahn, and Eddie Matthews, but there were some other 'greats' to say the least: Babe Ruth, Jim Thorpe, Rogers Hornsby, and Cy Young donned Braves' uniforms at points in their career. As of this writing, nearly fifty veterans of the Braves organization have been inducted into the Baseball Hall of Fame.

One could claim that the reason there is professional sports in Atlanta is because of the mayor at the time, Ivan Allen Jr., who in the mid-1960s supported building a stadium, even though the city had no team. *If you build it they will come...* As rumors spread about which team Atlanta may get, Milwaukee stomped its feet, crossed its arms, and said, "Un-uuh, the Braves aren't leaving our city!" According to the *St. Petersburg Times*, Milwaukee general manager John McHale said, "We have no commitment, verbal or otherwise, to anyone except Milwaukee to play baseball in 1965 or at any other time."

Months later, it was reported that the Braves organization had voted to move to Atlanta, but Milwaukee County officials weren't ready to throw in the towel just yet. After they voted to relocate, officials from Milwaukee acquired a court order preventing the Braves from changing cities. The National League halted the move in 1965, but cleared the way for the Braves relocation to Atlanta in 1966.

The Braves move to Atlanta was a groundbreaking event, but coming in fifth place in their division was not. The first three years were disastrous, even with an offense that included Hank Aaron, Joe Torre, Eddie Mathews, Rico Carty, and Felipe Alou. The 1969 season was the first sign of light for the Braves since leaving Wisconsin. Hosting two knuckleballers, Phil Niekro and Hoyt Wilhelm, and acquiring Orlando Cepeda, the stars seemed to align for the Braves. They won the West Division under manager Luman Harris, but they couldn't make it any further.

The Braves continued to struggle every year in the 1970s. That decade the team couldn't top third place in their division. Despite losing games, one of the most epic events in the history of baseball occurred when Hank Aaron surpassed Babe Ruth's home run record at Fulton County Stadium on April 8, 1974. Another crucial moment in Braves history occurred when the organization was purchased in 1976 by Ted Turner. According to *Braves Encyclopedia* author Gary Caruso, "Turner sat by the Braves dugout chewing tobacco, drinking beer and even taking off his shirt on hot afternoons. Among his stunts were sweeping off the bases between innings, participating in a motorized bathtub race, and pushing a baseball around the bases with his nose." He was willing to do anything to bring attention to his newly acquired team. Turner owned WTBS, Atlanta's channel 17, and eventually made the Braves a household name throughout the nation.

The late 1970s and early 1980s brought in new players and coaches. Dale Murphy and Bob Horner added a lift to the offense and Bobby Cox became manager in 1978. Turner, tired of losing, fired Cox after the 1981 season. Joe Torre stepped in and led the Braves to a first place finish with the help from Dale Murphy, Bob Horner, Chris Chambliss and Claudell Washington on offense, and Gene Garber, Rick Mahler, Phil Niekro, Steve Bedrosian, and Rick Camp at the mound. But like 1969, the Braves still couldn't make it past the West Division title.

The late 1980s brought a familiar Atlanta face: former Cracker Chuck Tanner became manager in 1986. The 1988 Braves were in a photo-finish with the Baltimore Orioles for the *&^%$# prize. *Use your imagination.* They were 54-106 in 1988, 63-97 in 1989, and 65-97 in 1990. The buck stops here! Bobby Cox was brought back as the Braves general manager in 1986, and he did some wheeling and dealing to build a team of biblical proportions. *Wait, want'n he fired?* That's right; Turner fired him as manager and rehired him in a higher position. *Guess ol' Teddy realized he made a mistake!* When Russ Nixon couldn't do any better than Tanner, Cox took over as manager and John Schuerholz secured his spot as general manager.

Bobby Cox and John Schuerholz made changes that led the Braves down the road of glory for more than a decade. The Braves won their division in 1991, but lost in the World Series against the Twins. The year 1991 saw the first of 14 consecutive division titles, a record-setting feat. The team made it to the World Series five times in the 90s, winning in 1995. The 1990s were the best decade the Braves (or most ball clubs) have ever seen. Bobby Cox retired after the 2010 season, ringing in a new era with Fredi Gonzalez calling the shots.

Legends

Hank Aaron (Braves)

Hammerin' Hank Aaron was born in Mobile, Alabama, on February 4, 1934. After playing ball in high school, he tried out for the Negro Leagues and played a year for the Indianapolis Clowns. The Milwaukee Braves recruited him in 1954, and he proved to the organization that they made probably the best decision in their long history. Eight seasons with 40 or more homeruns and 15 seasons with 30 or more is a feat that hardly happens in a ball player's career.

Hank Aaron played for 23 years in the majors. He started and ended in Milwaukee (moving on to the Brewers for his last two years.) As though he was born with a bat in his hand, he set numerous offensive records including total homeruns, RBIs, total bases, and extra base hits. His most memorable moment came in 1974 when he broke Babe Ruth's record of 714 career homeruns. As he rounded the bases, two fans rushed the field and ran with him. Aaron's teammates lifted him up and later he came out of the dugout to hug his wife.

He spent a lot of his time speaking out against the lack of minorities in office jobs for major-league teams. When his playing days were over he joined the Braves as executive vice-president. His homerun record was finally broken by Barry Bonds, but that is controversial, to say the least...

* **Hall of Fame (1982)**

* **All-Star: 1955-1975**

* **Batting Title: 1956, 1959**

* **MVP: 1957**

* **Gold Gloves: 1958, 1959, 1960**

AB	R	H	RBI	HR	2B	SB	BA
12364	2174	3771	2297	755	624	240	.305

Luke Appling (Georgia near-native)

Although born in North Carolina in 1907, Appling spent his youth in Atlanta. He went to Oglethorpe University in Brookhaven and played ball there for two years. It was at this time that he quit school and signed with the Atlanta Crackers. The Chicago White Sox bought his contract, and this is where he stayed for the rest of his twenty-year career.

His lifetime batting average of .310 is a testament to his excellent hitting ability. Able to keep his eye on the ball, he would foul balls off several times, leading to very long plate appearances. The *Milwaukee Journal* on August 12, 1949, wrote that "Luke has a knack of sloughing foul balls into the stands. He probably saved the major ball parks thousands of dollars by serving in the army a year and a half. He thinks nothing of fouling a dozen balls off in one time at bat."

Considering the longevity of his career, it's funny that he constantly complained about cramps or sprains throughout his career. He held nicknames like "Aches and Pains" and "Old Moaner," but he managed to set a record for the amount of games played at shortstop. Even at the age of seventy-five, he blew the crowd away when he hit a homerun off Warren Spahn's second pitch in the 1982 Old-Timers game. He was the oldest player on the team by close to ten years.

Appling spent many years after his retirement coaching in the minors and majors. On coaching, he said, "You'd think I'd get sick of saying the same things every day, but you can't give up on them. Some you pat on the back, some you kick on the butt."

* **Hall of Fame (1964)**

* **All-Star: 1936, 1939, 1940, 1941. 1943, 1946, 1947**

* **Batting Title: 1936, 1943**

* **Set record for number of games at shortstop (later broken)**

R	H	RBI	HR	2B	3B	SB	BA
1319	2749	1116	45	440	102	179	.310

Ralph "Country" Brown (Georgia native)

'Country' Brown was born on June 1, 1921, in Summerville, Georgia. He was probably the most popular player ever from the Atlanta Crackers. The funny part is that he was only on the team for just over three years.

He didn't play much baseball as a kid but realized his knack for it in the Army Air Force during World War II. While in the service, someone asked him where he came from and when he answered 'Summerville, Georgia', the man said, "That's what you are and that's where you are from ...the country." Before the discovery of his baseball talent he played football during his high school days in Chattooga County.

Early on, he spent time in Augusta with the Tigers and with the Tampa Smokers. He built quite a reputation in the Southern League, winning batting titles and making all-star appearances. When Brown was assigned to Montreal, he decided that he'd rather stay down South, announced his retirement, and went to work in a general store in Summerville. A short time later he returned to the Atlanta Crackers and finished the year as 'the Prince of Ponce de Leon'. After being suspended for insubordination and having conflicting personalities with the Crackers' manager, Dixie Walker, the team traded Brown to the Chattanooga Lookouts, after playing for more than three years in Atlanta.

Being a fan favorite and a top notch player, he surprisingly never played a game in the majors. He retired at the age of thirty-five due to eye floaters and knee problems, and then he moved back to his hometown, making a move into law enforcement. Eventually, he became a magistrate judge and served for more than two decades. Brown passed away on Christmas Eve 1996.

AB	R	H	RBI	HR	2B	3B	SB	BB	BA
6112	?	1882	?	116	356	108	?	?	.308

"Spud" Chandler (Georgia native)

Spurgeon Ferdinand Chandler, born in Commerce, Georgia, in 1907, was one of the greatest pitchers in the history of professional baseball. He made his start playing baseball for the University of Georgia, but he also excelled at track and dominated the football field. Furthermore, he graduated in 1932 with a degree in agriculture.

He spent several years in the minors until he finally got his start with the New York Yankees in 1937. There were articles during his day that exclaimed he wasn't a high-caliber pitcher, but he still managed to make it to the top. W.C. Heinz of the *Milwaukee Journal* wrote, "Of Chandler it might be said that a lot of pitchers who were given a lot more never went half as far." Apparently, Chandler was no natural, but he worked tirelessly and studied other pitchers which gave him that edge to greatness. He naturally had a fastball, but, Heinz wrote, "added through hours of hard work...a slider, ...screwball, ...forkball, and what he learned by studying the rest of the league would have made fine reference reading for any pitching staff in the circuit."

Chandler spent eleven years in the majors, all with the Yankees. He never had a losing season, and has the highest winning percentage of pitchers with more than 100 wins. In addition, he won the MVP in 1943 (fellow Georgian Luke Appling ranked second in the voting), and is the only Yankee pitcher to accomplish that feat. Accordingly, he was inducted into the Georgia Sports Hall of Fame in 1969 and the University of Georgia Ring of Honor in 2000.

He retired from playing professionally after the 1947 season and went on to coach, manage, and scout for the majors and minors for almost forty years. In 1990, he passed away in South Pasadena, Florida.

* **AL- MVP- 1943**

* **All-Star: 1942, 1943, 1946, 1947**

* **World Series: 1941, 1943, 1947**

W	L	ERA	CG	SHO	IP	BB	SO
109	43	2.84	109	26	1485	463	614

Ty Cobb (Georgia native)

The Georgia Peach is often considered the best baseball player of all time. Cobb was born in Royston, Georgia on December 18, 1886. He set hundreds of records when he played and many of them still stand —like a hefty .366 career batting average. While he was spectacular on the field, he was a spectacle off the field. Many consider that his antics were not as bad as they were made out to be. Apparently, his biographer, Al Stump, didn't get along well with Cobb and often portrayed him in a negative light.

Of course, it's easy to believe many of the incidents that Stump wrote about, considering that Cobb's exploits were often witnessed by thousands. In one such instance, the *Pittsburgh Press* reported in 1912 that, "Cobb was coming to bat…when a spectator in the grandstand let loose some epithets at him. As there is no police protection to take care of the players Cobb took matters in his hands and jumping over the low coop into the stand, delivered a series of stiff uppercuts and swings to the disturber's face, which brought blood freely."

Sometimes the harassment could be the other way around. According to the September 17, 1915, issue of the *New York Times*:

> Boston vented its ill felling on Ty Cobb. Each time that the Georgian came to bat he was booed and hissed and when the game was over the bleacherites made a rush at him. He became the center of a swirling crowd. Wads of paper were hurled at the Detroit player and heavier objects might have followed had not the police succeeded in working their way through the crowd of fans.

Getting his start in the South Atlantic League with the Augusta Tourists, Cobb moved on to play with the Detroit Tigers at the age of 18. Besides his rookie year, he never hit below .300 in a twenty four year career. He hit over .400 three times and over .350 sixteen times.

* **Batting Title:** '07, 08,09,11, 12, 13, 14, 15, 17, 18, 1919

R	H	RBI	HR	2B	3B	SB	BA
2245	4189	1938	117	724	284	897	.366

Tom Glavine (Braves)

"There are times I wish I could throw 100 miles an hour. 'Here it is. Go ahead and hit it.' But at the same time, it's fun seeing a guy gear up for a 3-2 fastball and just swing at what he thinks is a fastball, missing a changeup by a foot."

Thomas Michael Glavine, born in Concord Massachusetts on March 25, 1966, is truly a man of many talents. Not only was he drafted by the Atlanta Braves, but the National Hockey League's Los Angeles Kings drafted Glavine as well. The world will never know if he would have made as big a mark in hockey as he did in baseball. His career started in 1987 when he and the Braves were in their 1980s slump phase. Both the Braves and Glavine turned it around in 1991, when the Braves reached the World Series for the first time in over thirty years, and Glavine recorded twenty wins that season. In 1995, he was the World Series MVP.

Glavine also represented the Braves for the Major League Baseball Players Association. He made airtime on national television numerous times during the 1994 strike. Glavine has been involved in charities that have benefited the homeless, children with cancer, and transplant candidates.

* **Cy Young Award: 1991, 1998**

* **All Star: 1991, 92, 93, 96, 97, 98, 2000, 02, 04, 06 (10x)**

* **Silver Slugger: 1991, 1995, 1996, 1998**

* **National League Wins Leader: 1991, '92, '93, '98, 2000**

W	L	ERA	CG	SHO	SO
305	203	3.54	56	25	2607

Chipper Jones (Braves)

Larry Wayne Jones did something that most major league players don't do anymore: he played his entire nineteen-year career with one organization. Born in Deland, Florida in 1972, he went on to become the Braves' first pick in the 1990 draft. Jones played the next few seasons in the minors with Macon, Durham, Greenville, and Richmond. He played briefly in 1993 and had a batting average of .667. *No way!* Well ...he had two hits in three at-bats!

Jones played in a three World Series and was National League MVP in 1999. Constant injuries prevented him from reaching as many at-bats as he probably would have liked throughout the 2000s. He finished career on a high note, as a 2012 All-Star.

* **All Star – 1996, 1997, 1998, 2000, '01, '08, '11, 2012**

* **MVP – 1999**

* **Batting Title – 2008**

R	H	RBI	HR	2B	3B	SB	BA
1619	2726	1623	468	549	38	150	.303

Greg Maddux (Braves)

Maddux was picked in the second round of the 1984 draft by the Chicago Cubs. After a couple of years in their farm system, the Cubbies called him up and he began playing at the end of the 1986 season. In 1988, he started his streak of seventeen consecutive years with fifteen or more wins. He is the only pitcher in the history of Major League baseball to achieve such an accomplishment.

When he signed a five-year deal with the Braves in 1992, he was coming off a Cy Young-winning season. He would win it again in his first three seasons with the Braves. The Professor had back-to-back seasons with an ERA under 2.00 (1.56 and 1.63), and, to top it off, he also led the league in complete games in 1993, 1994, and 1995. There is no doubt that "Mad Dog" Maddux will go to the Hall of Fame in his first year of eligibility.

* **All-Star: 1988, 1992, 1994, 1995, 1996, 1997, 1998, 2000**

* **Cy Young: 1992, 1993, 1994, 1995**

* **Pitching Title: 1993, 1994, 1995, 1998**

W	L	ERA	CG	SHO	SO
355	227	3.16	109	35	3371

Eddie Mathews (Braves)

Mathews was born in Texarkana, Texas, on October 13, 1931. "Cap'n" Eddie played for two Atlanta teams in his career. *How's that possible?* Long before he was hitting homeruns as an Atlanta Brave, he started out as an Atlanta Cracker, and even helped them win the pennant. In that year he batted .286, hit 32 home runs, and 106 RBIs. Ty Cobb once said of Mathews, "I've known three or four perfect swings in my time. This boy's got one of them."

He ended up hitting over 20 homeruns in his rookie season with the Boston Braves. When the Braves moved to Milwaukee, Mathews received the nickname, "Milwaukee Mauler". *Oh, I get it; he was also a serial killer* —. With Aaron, Spahn, and Mathews as the leaders, the Braves won the World Series in 1957. After the franchise moved to Atlanta in 1966, Mathews became the only baller to play in all three Braves' cities.

On his retirement, he came back to Atlanta to help coach the Braves. He would eventually become the manager and he just happened to be there the day that Aaron hit his 715th homer. As a result of years of offensive dominance, he was inducted into the Hall of Fame in 1978. Throughout the 1980s he worked as a scout, hitting instructor, and held various coaching jobs. Matthews passed away in 2001.

* **Hall of Fame (1978)**

* **All Star: 1953, 55, 56, 57, 58, 59, 60, 61, 1962**

* **Home Run Titles: 1953, 1959**

AB	R	H	RBI	HR	2B	3B	BA
8537	1509	2315	1453	512	354	72	.271

Johnny Mize (Georgia native)

The city of Demorest, Georgia, proudly claims Hall of Famer Johnny Mize as one of their own, considering he was born there in 1913. He played baseball locally at Piedmont College in 1928, at the age of fifteen. The "Big Cat" started his professional career with the St. Louis Cardinals, but also played for the New York Giants and the Yankees. To end on a high note, he wrapped up his career helping the Yankees win five consecutive World Series.

It's one thing to talk about the 'big-time' accomplishments like homeruns and RBIs, but sometimes it's what a player doesn't do that is the real accomplishment. Mize had such control that he set records for lacking sttikeouts. Many power hitters "swing for the fences" and end up striking out a third of the time. He was patient and destructive at the same time. Mize had 524 strikeouts in 6,443 at-bats in his career (8 percent). To put that into perspective with another great player, Mickey Mantle had 1,710 strikeouts in 8101 at-bats (21 percent)

Mize could have easily hit a hundred more career homeruns if it weren't for World War II. He missed three years due to service in the Navy. After he retired from baseball he went on to coach for the Athletics and scout for the Giants. Coincidentally, he passed away where he started, in Demorest, Georgia, in 1993.

* **Hall Of Fame (1981)**

* **All Star: 1937, 1939, 1940, 1941, 1942, 1946, 1947, 1948, 1949, 1953**

* **Batting Title: 1939**

* **Hit three homeruns in a game six times (record)**

AB	R	H	RBI	HR	2B	3B	BB	BA
6443	1118	2011	1337	359	367	83	856	.312

Dale Murphy (Braves)

Murphy was born in Portland, Oregon, on March 12, 1956. After starting out at catcher, then moving to first base, he finally settled in the outfield. His first years were riddled with errors, but when he found himself in the outfield, he won five consecutive Gold Gloves. Winning back-to-back MVP awards wasn't too shabby either. Murphy's hitting prowess earned him four Silver Slugger awards in 1982, 1983, 1984, and 1985, and the Roberto Clemente Award for sportsmanship. His hitting started to decline and the Braves decided to trade Murphy to the Phillies in 1990. He spent his last year in Colorado and retired in 1994.

Murphy was known for his clean-living off the field, and he set an example for the younger players on his teams. He has worked with numerous charities and is a devout Mormon. The Braves retired his number 3 in 1994.

* **All Star: 1980, 1982, 1983, 1984, 1985, 1986, 1987**

* **MVP: 1982, 1983**

* **Gold Gloves: 1982, 1983, 1984, 1985, 1986**

AB	R	H	RBI	HR	2B	SB	BA
7960	1197	2111	1266	398	350	161	.265

Phil Niekro (Braves)

"I work for three weeks to get my swing down pat." Pete Rose once said, "and Phil messes it up in one night."

Phil Niekro is known for one major specialty ...his glorious hair. Oh yeah, and apparently he's one of the best knuckle ballers in the history of baseball. Phil and his brother Joe were taught this pitch by their dad, Joe Niekro Sr. There have been many quotes by baseball greats that detail just how difficult it was to try and hit a Niekro knuckle ball. Bobby Murcer said, "Trying to hit Niekro is like trying to eat Jell-O with chopsticks." Rick Monday stated, "It giggles as it goes by."

Niekro played ball for twenty-four seasons. Part of the reason he lasted so long in the majors is the fact that the knuckleball is easy on the arm. He led the league in wins while the Braves had the worst record in their division in 1979. As a matter of fact, he led the league in more than ten categories that year ...even losses. Even more impressive is that he led the Braves to the 1982 National League Championship at forty-three years old. His record was 17-4 that year. Niekro's gray hairs were coming out the sides of his hat while he was still striking out players half his age.

He finally retired after the 1987 season and went on to coach a women's team in Colorado. The Braves retired his number 35 in 1984, and later, the Braves placed a statue of Niekro at Turner Field, their home field in Atlanta. Niekro became a member of the Hall of Fame in 1997.

* **Hall of Fame (1997)**

* **All Star: 1969, 1975, 1978, 1982, 1984**

* **Pitching Title: 1967**

W	L	ERA	CG	SHO	IP	SO
318	274	3.35	245	45	5404	3342

Jackie Robinson (Georgia native)

Jackie Robinson is known for his baseball ability, and for breaking down the color barrier that existed in major-league baseball. Born in Cairo, Georgia, in 1919, he attended UCLA, and lettered in baseball, football, track, and basketball. After a stint in the military, Branch Rickey, president of the Brooklyn Dodgers, signed Robinson to the team in 1946.

His first year in the majors started in 1947 and was filled with every racist act one could think of. Robinson was cool and collected; he responded in silence, taking the high road. He became Rookie of the Year, an All-Star six times, and later an MVP. His number 42 has been retired by every major league team.

When he played an exhibition game against the Macon Peaches, he said:

> The best reception I got on the entire tour was in Macon. It proved to me then and there that Georgia sport fans are no different from any other. All sports fans are alike regardless of what section of the country they come from. The Macon fans came out to see a baseball game. They wanted entertainment, whether it was provided by a white person or Negro did not matter.

A few days later he would play in Atlanta against the Crackers, the *Associated Press* reported: "There was some spotty booing at first. But they were quickly drowned out by cheers from the majority of some 18,000 fans who came out to watch the first Negro ever to play here with a white against another white team…thousands stood up and applauded when Robinson [hit] a single over the second baseman's head."

* **Hall of Fame (1962)**

* **All-Star: 1949, 1950, 1951, 1952, 1953, 1954**

* **Batting Title and MVP: 1949**

R	H	RBI	HR	2B	3B	SB	BA
947	1518	734	137	273	54	197	.311

John Smoltz (Braves)

"Smoltzy" was born in Detroit, Michigan, in 1967, and was part of the Braves' pitching triumvirate of the 1990s. He began his career as a starter and would compile 213 wins over his twenty-one-year career. In 1996, his record of 24-8 earned him the Cy Young Award.

He suffered numerous injuries that caused him to miss several starts over the years, so he made a career altering decision: Smoltz became a closer (and led the league in saves in 2002). After 154 saves, he became a starting pitcher again. He holds the Atlanta Braves strikeout record with 3,084 (including his time with Boston and St. Louis) and is the only pitcher to reach more than 200 wins and 150 saves.

After retiring from baseball in 2009, he has been busy doing color commentary on Peachtree TV. He was inducted to the Georgia Sports Hall of Fame and there's no doubt he'll be selected to the Baseball Hall of Fame soon.

HIGHLIGHTS

* **All Star: 1989, 1992, 1993, 1996, 2002, 2003, 2005, 2007**

* **Pitching Title: 1996, 2006**

W	L	ERA	CG	SHO	SO	Saves
213	155	3.33	55	16	3084	154

Frank Thomas (Georgia native)

"The Big Hurt" was born in Columbus, Georgia, in 1968, and played baseball at Columbus High School; they would win the state championship. He attended Auburn University on a football scholarship and he also played on their baseball team. Thomas stuck with baseball and was the seventh pick in the draft by the Chicago White Sox. For seven straight years, Thomas hit above .300, had more than one hundred runs, RBIs, walks, and more than twenty home runs ...a major league record.

He wasn't the best defensively, so he made the switch to designated hitter after playing several years at first base. His ferocious power allowed him to set franchise records in home runs, RBIs, doubles, and several other categories. Thomas also advocated testing ball players for steroid use. The White Sox retired Thomas' number 35 in 2010.

HIGHLIGHTS

* **All Star: 1993, 1994, 1995, 1996, 1997**

* **MVP: 1993, 1994**

* **Batting Title: 1997**

AB	R	H	RBI	HR	2B	BB	BA
8199	1494	2468	1704	521	495	1667	.301

Notables

Felipe Alou

Felipe Alou was part of a family where "baseball" was everyone's middle name. His two brothers, Mattie and Jesus were also in the majors, and his son, Moises, had an excellent career as well. Felipe was named an All-Star three times, twice while in Atlanta. After retiring, he became a manager for the Expos and the Giants.

Steve Avery

Steve Avery was a member of the Braves "worst to first" club, and the nickname applied to him individually as well. His record of 3-11 in 1990 turned into 18-8 in 1991. The pinnacle of his career came when he was chosen as the NLCS MVP in 1991. In 1993, he made the All-Star team and finished the season with an 18-6 record. An injury during the 1993 season set a downward spiral for his career. In his rookie year of 1990, he was only twenty years old, so some might say that he had a lifetime of accomplishments before most people even start their careers.

The Bagby's

James Bagby Sr. was born in 1889, in Barnett, Georgia. The screwballer played nine seasons in the majors with the Reds, Indians, and Pirates. His had an overall record of 127-87 and a 3.10 ERA. In 1920, he won 31 games and helped the Indians win the pennant. James Bagby Jr. played for the Red Sox, the Indians, and the Pirates from 1938 to 1947. He was one of the pitchers to end Joe DiMaggio's hitting streak. Both he and his dad are members of the Georgia Sports Hall of Fame.

Dusty Baker

Although he has been credited with inventing high-five (seriously), Dusty Baker has some other accomplishments too. The Atlanta Braves drafted him in 1967 and he was in the outfield by 1968. He spent eight seasons with the Braves, although the first four years saw him come to bat 78 times. From 1972 to 1975, he was a quality starter, reaching double digit homeruns. Later in his career he would find success managing the Giants, the Cubs, and the Reds.

Bruce Benedict

Bruce Benedict emerged as the Braves' catcher in 1978 and stuck around until 1989. He made the All-Star teams in 1981 and 1983, and set an MLB record for throwing out three base runners in one inning. His lifetime batting average was .242, but his fielding percentage of .990 was phenomenal. *Not too shabby, Eggs.*

Jeff Blauser

Jeff Blauser was another player to be part of the "worst to first" phenomenon. He played shortstop for the Braves from 1987 to 1997. In his peak years, he was an All-Star in 1993 and 1997 and received the Silver Slugger award in 1997.

Sid Bream

Sid Bream (who was slow as dirt) scored from second base on a single by Francisco Cabrera, taking the Braves to the World Series in Game 7 of the NLCS in 1992. Bream's slide should be played in training videos around the world.

Rick Camp

Rick Camp pitched for the Braves his entire career, from 1976 to 1985. He was one of the worst-hitting pitchers in the game and managed to hit a home run in the eighteenth inning of a game against the Mets, his first and only home run. This turned out to be one of the most improbable homeruns in history. Unfortunately, he also did a stint in federal prison for conspiracy to commit fraud.

Skip Caray

The voice of the Braves, along with Pete Van Wieren, for many years, Skip Caray was the son of the famous announcer for the Cubs, Harry Caray. He began with the Braves in 1976 and Braves fans loved him for his sarcastic wit. Caray was inducted into the Georgia Sports Hall of Fame in 2013.

Rico Carty

Rico Carty dealt with injuries, tuberculosis, and major arguments with Braves teammates and coaches, but he was also one heck of a ball player. He was an All-Star in 1970, winning the batting title with a .366 average. Along with the Braves, Carty played on seven major league teams and finished his career with a .299 batting average.

Hugh Casey (native)

Known as "the Fireman," Hugh Casey was born in Atlanta on October 14, 1913, and started out with the Crackers. He played in the majors from 1935 to 1949 and compiled a 75-42 pitching record. In addition, he played for the Brooklyn Dodgers team that won the World Series in 1939. Casey also led the league in saves in 1942 and 1947 with the Dodgers and became a member of the Georgia Sports Hall of Fame in 1991.

Orlando Cepeda

Born on September 17, 1937, in Puerto Rico, Orlando Cepeda was a Brave from 1969 to 1972. He hit 74 homeruns and maintained a .281 batting average for three years in Atlanta. Unfortunately, his .455 batting average in the 1969 postseason wasn't enough to push the Braves through to the World Series. Eventually, the Braves traded him for veteran pitcher Denny McLain (the last pitcher to reach more than 30 wins) who didn't amount to much. Cepeda became a Hall of Famer in 1999.

Ellis Clary (native)

Ellis "the Cat" Clary was born in Valdosta, Georgia, in 1916, and he passed away there in 2000. He played for Washington and St. Louis during the war years and only hit one homerun in his MLB career. After his playing career, he went on to do some coaching and scouting. Clary was inducted into the Georgia Sports Hall of Fame in 1993.

Donn Clendenon (near native)

Although not born in Georgia, Donn Clendenon played high school ball in Atlanta and was later a star player for Morehouse College. He could have played football or basketball (he was even offered a contract from the Globetrotters), but opted to play baseball for the Pirates. Clendenon later played for the Mets, was the World Series

MVP in 1969, and became a member of the Georgia Sports Hall of Fame in 2005.

Claud Derrick (native)

Claud "Deek" Derrick was born in Burton, Georgia in 1886. He turned into an unbelievable player for the University of Georgia before going professional. In fact, he became the first person from UGA to make it to the majors. Derrick played for only five years with organizations that include the Phillies, the Yankees, the Reds, and the Cubs. Due to his mark on Georgia history, he was inducted into the Georgia Sports Hall of Fame in 1992.

Samuel 'Sambo' Elliott (native)

What!? What's a softball pitcher doing in here? This amazing fast-pitch softball pitcher threw 107 no-hitters during the 1930s, 1940s, and 1950s. His overall record was 1046-87 and he struck out 13,936 hitters. All that and he threw underhanded! Makes some of the pitchers in the majors seem, well, just plain awful. He was inducted into the Georgia Sports Hall of Fame in 1977.

Darrell Evans

Darrell Evans spent nine seasons in a Braves uniform, the last of which came in 1989 when he was forty-two years old. He led the league in walks in 1973 and 1974. Evans hit over 400 homeruns in his career, but his .248 career batting average damaged his chances of glory in the Hall of Fame. In 1973, he was part of the trio of Braves who hit forty or more homeruns, along with Dave Johnson and Hank Aaron.

Ron Gant

Ron Gant made his start with the Braves in 1987 and played there until 1993. In 1990 and 1991, he hit more than 30 homeruns and stole more than thirty bases. After signing a single-year contract with the Braves for over $5 million, he broke his leg in a four-wheeling accident. The Braves released him to save money, but Gant would go on to play several more years with the Reds, Cardinals, Phillies, Angels, Rockies, and the Athletics. In seven years with the Braves he hit 147 homers, had 157 stolen bases, and 600 strikeouts.

Gene Garber

In ten years with the Braves, 1978 to 1987, Gene Garber held an ERA of 3.34 and compiled 141 saves. He snapped Pete Rose's 44-game hitting streak in 1978 with a side-armed change-up, which was his specialty. Today, he lives on a farm in Pennsylvania with thousands of emus. Gene Garber: side-arm pitcher and emu oil salesmen. *Put that on your resume!*

Ralph Garr

Ralph Garr, "the Road Runner" played with the Braves from 1968 to 1975, averaging .317 in 800 games with the Atlanta organization. In 1974, he led the league in triples (17), hits (214), and won the batting title with a .353 batting average. He was traded in 1975 for Ozzie Osborn (*not what you're thinking*). In 1971, the Braves actually negotiated a deal with Warner Brothers (*Looney Toons*) to allow the animated Road Runner character on the scoreboard and to use the signature "beep-beep" noise each time Garr reached base.

Josh Gibson (native)

Hall of Famer Josh Gibson was often called the "black Babe Ruth". Although he never saw action in the Major League, Gibson will always be remembered for is catching abilities and slugging prowess in the Negro Leagues. He was born in Buena Vista, Georgia, in 1911 and died in 1947. It is stated on his Hall of Fame plaque that he hit close to 800 homeruns. During his career, he played for the Pittsburgh Crawfords and the Homestead Grays.

James Tolbert Hearn (native)

Born in Atlanta, on April 11, 1921, James Hearn started his career with the Cardinals in 1947. After playing for the Yellow Jackets, he entered World War II and then spent time in the minors. A pitcher, his overall record was 109-89 with 669 strikeouts and a 3.81 ERA. He was an All-Star in 1952 and is a member of the Georgia Sports Hall of Fame.

Bob Horner

With nine years as a Brave, from 1978 to 1986, Bob Horner hit twenty or more homeruns in seven seasons. After becoming MVP of the College World Series in 1977, he was the first pick in the 1978 amateur draft. Being totally awesome, he never set foot on a minor league baseball field, and, subsequently, won the National League Rookie of the Year award in 1978. He was an All-Star in 1982, and in 1986 became part of an elite club after hitting four homeruns in a game. Horner would later play a year of baseball in Japan, where he averaged one home run for every ten at-bats. He came back for a brief comeback in the MLB, but due to shoulder issues, he retired in 1989. He was inducted into the College Baseball Hall of Fame in 2006.

Glenn Hubbard

Glenn Hubbard was the Braves second baseman from 1978 to 1988, and wore one heck of a moustache. He was known for his excellent defensive skills and holds many Braves' records at second base. A renowned bunter, Hubbard led the league in 1982 with twenty sacrifice bunts. Later, he would be the first base coach for the Braves from 1999 to 2010.

Tim Hudson

Tim Hudson was born in 1975 in Columbus, Georgia, and became a star player at Auburn University. His major-league career began with the Oakland Athletics, and he made the All-Star team in 2000. The Athletics traded Hudson to the Braves in 2005, and he's been an All-Star twice since donning a red, white, and blue uniform. The sinker-baller wound up as Comeback Player of the Year in 2010, after undergoing Tommy John surgery. He's never had a winning percentage in a season below .520 and he has eight seasons with fifteen or more wins.

Pat Jarvis

Pat Jarvis started pitching for the Braves when they came to Atlanta, and in 1966, he was 6-2 in nine starts, with a 2.31 ERA. In seven seasons with the Braves he had 83 wins, 73 losses, and an ERA of 3.58. He later became sheriff of DeKalb County, Georgia, but was convicted of federal mail fraud in 1999 and sentenced to fifteen months in jail.

Dave Johnson

Although Davey Johnson only spent a few years with the Atlanta Braves, he made quite an impact. He was part of the record-breaking group of three that hit forty or more homeruns in a season on the same team (the others were Hank Aaron and Darrell Evans). Johnson was an All-Star four times, Gold Glove winner three times, and led the league in errors for a second baseman twice. *So he was good and bad at second base?* After his playing days, Johnson became a successful manager of multiple Major League teams, becoming Manager of the Year twice.

Ernie Johnson

Ernie Johnson was in broadcast television and radio for the Braves, from 1962 to 1999. The Braves inducted him into their Hall of Fame in 2001. Although he never played baseball for Atlanta, he played as a Brave in Boston and Milwaukee. After his death in 2011, the Braves wore commemorative patches on their uniforms.

Andruw Jones

Andruw Jones was the Braves' star outfielder for twelve years. Born in the Caribbean nation of Curacao, he worked his way to the majors and signed with the Braves at the age of sixteen. He went on to be an All-Star in 2000, 2002, 2003, 2005, and 2006 and won the Gold Glove ten years in a row starting in 1998. His career totals by 2012 were 434 home runs, 1,289 RBIs, 152 stolen bases, and a .254 batting average.

Brian Jordan

Brian Jordan is special to Atlanta because he was both a Brave and a Falcon. He played for the National Football League's Falcons from 1989 to 1991 and led the team in tackles in 1991. The safety and outfielder would end up playing for the Braves for five inconsecutive seasons compiling 71 homeruns, 323 RBIS, and 96 doubles in 1947 at-bats.

David Justice

David Justice was married to Halle Berry. *Why ...that ... son of a #@%^&!* He also took over Dale Murphy's position. *Why ...that ...son of a %$#^&.* He criticized fans for not being very supportive. *Why ...that ...son of a @#$%^.* Besides these tidbits of information, he actually had a solid career as a Braves outfielder for eight seasons. Justice was a three-time All-Star, two-time World Series champion (one as a Brave), and Rookie of the Year in 1990.

Ray Knight (native)

Ray Knight was born in Albany, Georgia, in 1952. He played in the majors from 1974 to 1988 for teams that include the Reds, Astros,

Mets, Orioles, and the Tigers. Not surprisingly, he was the World Series MVP for the Mets in 1986 after he scored the winning run in game six and the tiebreaking homer in game seven. The two-time All-Star was also Comeback Player of the Year in 1986.

Mark Lemke

Mark "the Lemmer" Lemke spent ten years with the Braves and was an excellent defensive second baseman. *That just means he couldn't hit!* More like be hit —he holds the major-league record for career at-bats without being hit by a pitch (3664). Lemke retired in 1998 and went on to be a sports radio personality.

Javier Lopez

Javier "Javy" Lopez played twelve years for the Braves as their catcher from 1992 to 2003. He was an All-Star in 1997, 1998, and 2003, not to mention being a part of the 1995 World Series win. Lopez was also the National League Championship Series MVP in 1996; he batted .542 with two homeruns.

Gary Matthews

Gary Matthews spent four years with the Braves, from 1977 to 1980, some of the worst years in the team's history. Although the Braves record was 277- 368 in the four years Matthews was on the scene, it had nothing to do with his performance. He hit .288, with 81 homeruns, 291 RBIs, and 59 stolen bases. During the 1979 season he was selected to the All-Star team, the only All-Star appearance of his career.

Brian McCann

As of this writing, McCann is a five-time Silver Slugger and six-time All-Star catcher for the Braves. He was part of a group of rookies who came up in 2005, and he has lasted the longest. Although there are many catchers out there with better defensive records, McCann has more than made up for that with his offensive ability. He averaged over twenty homeruns in his first seven full seasons in the majors.

Fred McGriff

Fred McGriff "the Crime Dog" replaced Sid Bream at first base in 1993 and stayed with the Braves for five seasons during their heyday of championship baseball. As a Brave, he accumulated 130 home runs, 446 RBIs, and batted .293. McGriff would go on to hit 493 home runs and reach 1,550 RBIs in his career. He was an All-Star five times and a Silver Slugger three times. It should also be mentioned that in 188 post season at-bats, he hit ten homeruns and batted .303.

Kent Mercker

Picked up by the Braves in 1986, Kent Mercker pitched for the Braves from 1989 to 1995, with a brief appearance in 2003 for eighteen games. Mercker took part in two no-hitters in his career with the Braves. He had a combined no-hitter with Mark Wohlers and Alejandro Pena in 1991. He pitched one on his own in 1994 against the Dodgers.

Felix Milan

Felix Milan, known as El Gatito ("the Kitten") ...*meow*... played with the original Atlanta Braves from 1966 to 1972. He was a Gold Glove winner for second base in 1969 and 1972, and made the All-Star team in 1969, 1970, and 1971. After the Braves traded him to the Mets, he got into an on-field fight with Ed Ott, in which Milan punched Ott, who retaliated by body slamming him to the ground and dislocating his shoulder. No more major-league baseball for Mr. Milan.

Bob Montag (near native)

His 113 homeruns for the Atlanta Crackers were the most in club history. Even though Montag never played a game in the majors, he had a fan base in the minors as though he was Mickey Mantle. He hit one home run at Poncey Park that left the stadium and landed in a passing train's coal car. His hitting helped the Crackers win the Dixie Series against the Houston Buffaloes, which included a homerun in game three of the series.

Red Moore (native)

Red Moore was a Negro League All-Star who played for the Newark Eagles, the Atlanta Black Crackers, Indianapolis ABCs, and the Baltimore Elite Giants. He was known for his defensive skills and behind-the-back catches during exhibition games.

Wallace Moses (native)

Wally Moses was born in Uvalda, Georgia in 1910 and died in Vidalia, Georgia, in 1990. He made the All-Star teams in 1937 and 1945, and played for the Athletics, White Sox, and Red Sox. His career batting average was .291, and he compiled 2,138 hits, 1,114 runs, 110 triples, and 174 stolen bases. In 1989 he was inducted into the Georgia Sports Hall of Fame.

Otis Nixon

Otis Nixon holds the Braves record for stolen bases in a season with 72, and he holds the record for most stolen bases in a game with six. Nixon struggled with drugs throughout his career, and after failing a drug test with the Braves, he couldn't play in the 1991 World Series. With four years for the Braves, he stole 186 bases, averaging more than 46 a season. He was skilled defensively and once robbed Andy Van Syke of a homerun by reaching over the wall to catch the ball. In 17 years in the majors, he stole 620 bases.

Willard Nixon (native)

Willard Nixon was born in Taylorsville, Georgia, in 1928, and played for the Boston Red Sox from 1950 to 1958. He had 51 complete games in his career and was also one of the best-hitting pitchers in the league. He was inducted into the Georgia Sports Hall of Fame in 1993.

John Odom (native)

John "Blue Moon" Odom was a two-time All-Star and three-time World Series champion. He played the majority of his career with the Athletics, but spent time in Cleveland, Atlanta, and Chicago. He led his high school in Macon, Georgia, to the state championships twice and pitched eight no-hitters. His ERA during playoff and World Series play was an unbelievable 1.13. He was inducted into the Georgia Sports Hall of Fame in 2004.

John C. Odom

John Odom was a pitcher who accumulated a 9-9 record and a 4.12 ERA in his minor league career. An excellent pitcher growing up, he played a little in college, and the Giants decided to draft him. Many know him for being traded for ten baseball bats, which was unheard of in baseball. Aside from his athletic ability, he was also considered a genuine guy with many friends and admirers. Unfortunately, he passed away at the young age of twenty-six due to a drug overdose.

Greg Olson

The odds were never in his favor, but the stars aligned and Greg Olson got his chance. With catching issues in the Braves organization becoming a problem, Olson took over behind the plate and remained there for four years. His picture will forever be etched in the minds of those who watched the clinching of the pennant, when he jumped into the arms of John Smoltz. He was an All-Star in 1990.

Nat Peeples (near native)

Nat Peeples was the only African American to play for the Atlanta Crackers, and the Southern Association Baseball League. Although brief, lasting only two weeks, in 1953 he signed with the Boston Braves and reported to the Atlanta Crackers. Earl Mann sent him down to the single-A club in Jacksonville. Some suggested the move was based on racism, while others suggested it was his skill level. He would never make it to the majors...

Terry Pendleton

Terry Pendleton was just what the Braves needed after a last place finish. He helped lead the Braves to the 1991 World Series, and in that year he won a Gold Glove, the National League batting title, the MVP, and was the Comeback Player of the Year. He made the All-Star team the following year too. After he retired, he took on a coaching job with the Braves.

Pascual Perez

"Perimeter" Pascual Perez only pitched as a Brave for a few seasons, but in 1983 and 1984 he had a combined record of 29-16. In 1985, he had a truly awful record of 1-13, and the Braves released him after that. Pascual is most famous for missing a start because he couldn't find Atlanta Fulton County Stadium. Apparently, he drove around the I-285 at least two times and had to stop and get gas. The funny part is that he had just obtained a driver's license that morning.

Gaylord Perry

Gaylord Perry pitched briefly with the Braves in 1981 near the end of his career. Perry's age of 43 didn't stop him from reaching eight wins. His 314 wins were enough to get him into the Hall of Fame in 1991. Perry, known for his "questionable" pitches, psyched out batters with his famous spitball and later the infamous "puffball."

Ron Reed

As the Braves began their new start in Atlanta in 1966, Ron Reed started right there with them. With the Braves, Reed pitched 80 wins, a 3.74 ERA, and 47 complete games. He was selected as an All-Star in 1968 and helped the Braves win their division in 1969.

Elmer Riddle (native)

Elmer was born in Columbus, Georgia on July 31, 1914. He pitched for the Reds and Pirates from 1939 to 1950 and was an All-Star in 1948. With his help, the Reds became the 1940 World Series Champions. In 1994, Riddle was inducted into the Georgia Sports Hall of Fame.

John Rocker

The notorious John Rocker came on the scene for Atlanta as the outspoken relief pitcher from Statesboro, Georgia. He accumulated 332 strikeouts in less than 256 innings. After working a few solid seasons as the Braves' closer, his off-the-field remarks got the best of him. In an interview with *Sports Illustrated,* he offended about every single ethnic group when discussing why he wouldn't want to live in New York City. He now sells T-shirts that say "Speak English". *Go figure...*

Jerry Royster

Before Chipper Jones and Ken Oberkfell, third base was occupied by Jerry Royster. Royster was known for his base running abilities and would usually lead-off in the lineup. After playing with the Braves from 1976 to 1984, he came back for a year in 1988, then retired that year. He went on to coach and manage teams in the minors.

Nap Rucker (native)

George Napoleon Rucker was born in 1884 in Crabapple, Georgia. He pitched for the Brooklyn Superbas and once threw a no-hitter against the Boston Doves. After his fastball began to decline he started using the knuckleball, which gives pitchers longevity. He later became the mayor of Roswell, Georgia, in 1935. His nephew Johnny was a graduate of the University of Georgia and played professional baseball for six years in the 1940s. Johnny also went by the "Crabapple Comet."

Harry L. Simpson (native)

Harry L. "Suitcase" Simpson was born in Atlanta in 1925 and played in the majors from 1951 to 1959 for the Indians, Athletics, Yankees, White Sox, and Pirates. Before his stint in the majors, he played in the Negro Leagues with the Philadelphia Stars from 1946 to 1948. After his days in the majors, he spent time with some minor league clubs and ended his career playing in the Mexican League. He was an All-Star in 1956 and twice led the league in triples.

Sherrod Smith (native)

Sherrod Smith was born in Monticello, Georgia, in 1891. He pitched fourteen years in the majors with the Pirates, Dodgers, and the Indians. With 114 career wins, a 3.32 ERA and 142 complete games, he was an easy selection in the 1980 Georgia Sports Hall of Fame induction. After his playing career, he coached for a few teams, one being the Macon Peaches.

Warren Spahn

Warren Spahn never actually pitched for Atlanta, but deserves to be mentioned in this book because he played for both the Boston and Milwaukee Braves, not to mention his killer leg kick. He won 363 games, struck out 2,583 batters, and won a Cy Young Award in 1957. His number 21 was retired by the Atlanta Braves. Spahn once said, "Hitting is timing. Pitching is upsetting timing."

George Stallings (native)

George Stallings was born in Atlanta (coincidentally the city where his Boston team would end up) and went on to achieve over 800 wins as a major league manager. He took over the managerial position for the last place Boston Braves in 1913. In 1914 he led the Braves to a World Series win against the Philadelphia Athletics.

Chuck Tanner

Best of the Crackers and worst of the Braves... Chuck Tanner's career began as an Atlanta Cracker, where he played for four seasons and held his batting average above .300. He helped the Crackers win the Dixie Series against the Houston Buffaloes in 1954. After playing several years in the majors, he retired and began his life as a major league manager. Tanner was Manager of the Year in 1972 and led the Pirates to a World Series win in 1979. He took over the Braves in

1986, but it seemed there was no helping them at this point. As a result, the Braves fired him after two seasons.

Joe Torre

Joe Torre's career began with the Braves franchise in Milwaukee. As a Brave he played nine seasons and hit .294, hit 142 home runs, and had over 1,000 hits. After his playing career was over, he became one of the best managers of all time. He replaced Bobby Cox as the manager for the Braves and led them to the division title in 1982. The Braves record started dropping, and he was let go after a few years. Torre would go on to manage the Yankees and take them to unbelievable heights.

Cecil Travis (native)

Cecil Travis was born in Riverdale, Georgia, in 1913. He played for the Washington Senators from 1933 to 1947. The hero missed almost four complete seasons due to service in World War II, for which he received a Bronze Star. The three-time All-Star's career batting average was .314, and he had over 1,500 hits in 4,914 at-bats. Not surprisingly, he was inducted into the Georgia Sports Hall of Fame in 1975.

Bob Uecker

Bob Uecker might be best known as George in the TV show *Mr. Belvedere*, and as the sportscaster in the *Major League* movies. He was actually a ball player, and not only that, he was a ball player for the Braves. Uecker didn't play too much, but he did catch for Phil Niekro and once said about the best way to catch for him was to "wait till it stops rolling, walk over, and pick it up."

Cecil Upshaw

Pitcher Cecil Upshaw was one of the better relievers in the majors in the late 1960s and early 1970s. As a Brave, he had a career ERA of 3.01, 78 saves, and a 30-26 record. After seven seasons with the Braves, he played for the Astros, Indians, Yankees, and the White Sox.

Jo Jo White (native)

Joyner, "Jo-Jo" White was born in Red Oak, Georgia, in 1909. He played with the Detroit Tigers, Philadelphia Athletics, and the Cincinnati Reds off and on from 1932 to 1944. Early in his career, he was part of the Tiger's World Series win in 1935. After his playing days ended, he coached for the Milwaukee/Atlanta Braves.

Ivey Wingo (native)

Ivey Wingo was born in 1890 in Gainesville, Georgia. He played from 1911 to 1929 with a couple of years missing near the end of his career. Luckily, he was part of the winning Reds team against the notorious 1919 White Sox in the World Series. He died at only 50 years old in 1941 and was inducted into the Georgia Sports Hall of Fame in 1993.

Mark Wohlers

Mark Wohlers had one of the fastest pitches in baseball history; he was once clocked at 103 mph. He was the Braves set-up man and closer for nine years. His Atlanta record was 31-22, with a 3.73 ERA, and 437 strikeouts in 386.1 innings. Wohlers had three solid seasons as the team's closer and totaled 112 saves as a Brave. He also took part in a no-hitter with Kent Mercker and Alejandro Pena.

Whitlow Wyatt (native)

Whit Wyatt was born in Kensington, Georgia, in 1907 and had a sixteen-year career as a major-league pitcher. He became the manager of the Atlanta Crackers and led them to the Dixie Series in 1954. Later on, he left the minor leagues to act as pitching coach for the Phillies and the Braves.

Rudy York (native)

Rudy York played major-league ball for more than a decade in the 1930s and 40s. He is widely known for hitting eighteen home runs in a month, beating Babe Ruth's record. Although born in Alabama, he moved to Cartersville, Georgia, as a boy. With four seasons hitting more than thirty homeruns, York could hit the ball hard to say the least. After retiring from the majors in 1948, he held several minor-league coaching positions.

Coaches and Notables

Earl Mann

Earl Mann, "Mr. Atlanta Baseball" started out selling peanuts and ended up owning the most successful Southern baseball organization in the minor leagues. He represented the American dream of working oneself up the ladder to success.

After his peanut-vending days, he began selling tickets to Crackers games. He became assistant team secretary, and then the secretary. After a few years managing other teams he became the vice president of the Atlanta Crackers before the age of thirty. He then became the team's president and owner at the age of forty.

Before the Braves, the Crackers were Atlanta's team, and he was Atlanta's baseball savior. The Crackers won more championships than anyone else in professional baseball (yeah, yeah, besides the Yankees).

Bobby Cox

What's better than holding the record for most ejections as a manager? ...Nothing.

Bobby Cox was born in Tulsa, Oklahoma in 1941, but he will always be considered an Atlanta man by all the metro residents. He played in the Dodger farm system for several years and played a season for the Yankees. Though playing third base didn't make him famous, sitting in the dugout did.

His managerial career began in the Yankees farm system where he compiled a .543 winning percentage over six years. After a stint as the first-base coach for the 1977 Yankees, he took over as manager in Atlanta. It was not an easy endeavor, considering he was taking over a last-place team, but he did the best he could with the hand he was dealt. He brought them above .500 in 1980, but Ted Turner fired him after the 1981 season. The Braves won their division the following year, and some said it was Cox's build-up of the team that got them there.

He managed the Blue Jays for the next four years, culminating in the American League Championship. Cox was hired again by the Braves in 1985 as the general manager, and successfully built the team from the ground up. He acquired such players as Steve Avery, Tom Glavine, and Chipper Jones. After firing Russ Nixon in the middle of the 1990 season, he took over as manager. In 1991, he decided to stay on in the job, and John Schuerholz became GM.

The year 1991 was the beginning of a magical journey for Cox, the Braves, and fans all over Georgia and the United States. The Braves won their division fourteen years in a row; they also won five pennants, and one World Series. Cox is fourth on the all-time wins record list (2,504-2,001), the most wins in Braves franchise history. He holds another record that many consider his best: the one for the most ejections …158 in regular-season play. It's been said that many of these were to prevent players from being tossed. A class act all the way. The Braves retired his jersey and he is in the Georgia Sports Hall of Fame.

Ted Turner

Born in 1938, Ted Turner took his father's billboard business to new levels and became a billionaire in the process. Along the way, he bought the Atlanta Braves and the Atlanta Hawks, taking them to new heights too.

Turner bought the Braves in 1976 and a majority of shares of the Hawks a short time later. He used his TBS station to broadcast games live and gained a nationwide following. He is also known for the Goodwill Games, Captain Planet, Ted's Montana Grill, TNT, CNN, colorizing old movies, numerous off-the-wall comments, owning more US land than would cover the state of Delaware, and marrying Jane Fonda. A skilled yachtsman, he was inducted into the National Sailing Hall of Fame in 2011.

What was the name of Chief
Noc-a-Homa's assistant?
Princess Win-a-Lotta

<u>5</u>

— Football —

Way Back When

The Flying Wedge

The Roman Legions are outnumbered and attempting to put down a revolt. They use the flying wedge to pierce into the enemy's formation. Success! *Well, golly, why can't this be used in sports?* Well, it could for a brief period in the late 1800s, and it was very successful —but brutal, causing many injuries, and in some instances, death. It was banned in 1894.

Don't touch Me There

Early on, football players wore little protective gear, so the rules of contact were nothing like they are today. Below the waist and above the shoulders were off limits.

20 Versus 20

Each team had twenty players on the field …chaos. Walter Camp can be credited for knocking that number down to 11.

Red Rover

Players locked arms and ran downfield providing an extensive shield for the ball carrier. There's an accident waiting to happen.

Third Down

At first, there were no downs. Another one of Walter Camp's changes in 1882 was the down system: three downs to reach five yards. Thirty years later, fourth down was added.

A Kicking Game

Field goals were worth five points and touchdowns were worth four points.

The Forward Pass

Before the forward pass became legal in 1906, an incomplete pass would cost the offense fifteen yards, and a completed pass caught in the end zone was a touchback. *Huh?*

History

Here's the myth: some youngins' were playing soccer and one of the more wily players got frustrated. He picked up the ball and started running with it. The other players got pissed that he's making a mockery of the game, so a chase ensued. Finally, they caught up and tackled him. A new game is born! *Wow, is that really how it all started? Yes, Timmy, and a stork brought you to your parents when you were a baby.*

Basically, rugby was played on school campuses and by the youth about town, and then some key changes to the game made it functionally different. Different schools had particular rules, like the Princeton rules, Rutgers rules, Boston rules, and so on. There was an attempt to standardize the rules in 1873, with Harvard not attending because the other schools wouldn't allow carrying the ball. When Harvard played McGill University of Montreal, they enjoyed the "try" goal that McGill used. The try is equivalent to a touchdown. *Got it.* This would become the new standard, for a while.

Walter Camp from Yale made football close to what it is today. He remained part of the rule committee until his death in 1925. Camp played football for Yale and later coached them for five years. His lifetime coaching record (including three years with Stanford) was 79-5-3. *Not bad, especially when you make the rules!*

The following are a number of the changes made while Camp was on the annual rules committee:

- Number of players decreased from 15 to 11
- The line of scrimmage
- The snap (Heisman)
- Down and distance limits
- Reduction of the field size to today's size
- Adding more points for a touchdown
- Adding a referee and an umpire

College Football

Looking at football today, you might think the game started in the South. You'd be wrong. The first game of collegiate "foot-ball" was held between Princeton and Rutgers on November 6, 1869. ...*It's a Jersey thing.* The game was more a combination between rugby and soccer back then. It took a few years before it took hold in Georgia. In an 1887 article for *Century Magazine* called "The American Game of Foot-Ball", Alexander Johnston wrote that "the game has found little favor at the South, but almost every Northern college now plays it more or less."

The biggest games of this era were between Princeton and Yale. A lot has changed in 125 years.

Football had somewhat of a difficult start in the South, partially due to religious fervor. Bishop Warren Akin Candler banned football (and the drama club) at Emory University. According to "No More Football," a November 1897 article in the *Atlanta Journal,* the game was thought to be on its way out: "The game has been tried and justly condemned as brutal, cruel, and dangerous. It is not an American game anyway. It is an importation from England and one that has done more harm than good." Although religion played a part of prohibiting football in private institutions, it was injury and death that caused the most uproar from the public and politicians.

The game in its early days was rough, to say the least. In terms of pads and equipment, it may have well been a street game between the kids from Lord of the Flies. In terms of toughness, it puts a little perspective on the ruggedness of the players of then and now. A recap on a game between Augusta and Athens in the *Red and Black* from 1893, reported, "In a scrimmage Smith has his nose broken and face badly bruised. He is plucky and in a few minutes enters the play again." It's difficult to imagine any player today with that sort of bravado.

Football was not the first intercollegiate competitive sport in the United States. The first college competition was a rowing meet between Harvard and Yale; row, row, row your boat. Harvard won! *Whoop-de-doo...*

UGA Football

"I'm Bulldog born, Bulldog bred, and when I die, I'll be by-God Bulldog dead."
— Lewis Grizzard

Football at the University of Georgia came into being in 1892, with Georgia beating Mercer 50-0. *Not a bad start.* Who gave UGA its first football team? *It was probably some grizzly old coach who was making men out of boys.* Not exactly. A chemistry professor by the name of Charles Herty developed the college's first football team. He also developed a new system for collecting turpentine from pine trees and a new way to transform wood pulp into paper down in Savannah. With a 10-0 loss against Auburn as the team's second game in history, a rivalry that still causes fighting words among friends and family to this day began.

The next couple of decades brought about an event that would forever change football in Georgia and the rest of the nation. A new young quarterback named Von Gammon experienced a life-ending injury on the field in 1897. The *Athens Banner* a few days after Gammon's untimely death reported, "Football in Georgia is a thing of the past. The gridiron is deserted and the pigskin has been laid away. There will be no more of this brutality witnessed on Georgia soil."

Legislation banning football was vetoed by Gov. William Atkinson and he gave multiple reasons for his decision. On December 9, 1897, the *Athens Daily Banner* quoted the governor:

> Football causes less deaths than hunting, boating, fishing, horseback riding, bathing or bicycling. If we are to engage in legislation of this character now under discussion, the state should assume the position of parent, forbid all these sports to boys, make it a penal offense for a boy to engage in any of them and for any parent to permit his child to engage in them. Every possible facility should be afforded boys and young men in all our schools and colleges to engage in such manly sports as will upbuild, strengthen and improve our race."

Even Gammon's mother wrote to the governor pleading that the game not end in the name of her son. Thus, the game goes on.

Years later, Coach W.A. Cunningham led UGA to seven winning seasons between 1910 and 1919. The team disbanded in 1917 and 1918, considering most of their able-bodied men were fighting in the Great War. During these years, the playing field was switched to the newly constructed Sanford Field, and in 1929 the thirty-thousand-seat Sanford Stadium was completed with funds from alumni and fans in return for "lifetime seats".

After about a .660 winning percentage under coaches Herman J. Stegeman, "Kid" Woodruff, and Harry Mehre, UGA spent the next twenty-two years under the tutelage of Wally Butts. Under Butts, the Bulldogs record was 140-86-9. The team won the National Championship in 1942. Since the next couple of seasons were interrupted by World War II, one may wonder what might have been. After four SEC championships, Butts retired in 1960.

Starting in 1964, the next twenty-five years held the longest lasting coach in Bulldogs history, Vince Dooley. UGA won the National Championship for the second time in 1980 with a little help from their new star running back, Herschel Walker. With Dooley behind the wheel, the team's record was 201-77-10, with six SEC championships.

From 1989 to 2000 the Bulldogs went through coaches Ray Goff and Jim Donnan and won no conference titles. In 2001, UGA was able to grab Mark Richt from the Florida State Seminoles, and his 100-plus wins and two SEC championships have been a blessing to the Dawgs.

Team Highlights

◉ **Athens, Georgia**

◉ **Founded: 1785- First season: 1892**

◉ **Conference: Southeastern Conference**

◉ **Nickname: Bulldogs**

◉ **Colors: Red and Black**

- SEC Championships: 1942, 1946, 1948, 1959, 1966, 1968, 1976, 1980, 1981, 1982, 2002, 2005

- Main Rivals: Florida, Auburn (oldest), Georgia Tech (and all other SEC teams)

- No Kiddin'? – The original mascot was a goat

Legends
Champ Bailey

Ronald "Champ" Bailey is one of the few players who really deserve his nickname. The cornerback was born in Folkston, Georgia, on June 22, 1978. After finishing high school with the Charlton County Indians, he played for UGA from 1996 to 1998. With his versatility, he was explosive on offense, defense, and special teams. He is considered one of the best all-around players in the game. His time at Georgia was more than in demand. An article in the *Red and Black* from October 9, 1998 puts it into perspective:

> Defensive coordinator Kines wants to see <him>…about defensive assignments … Donnan needs to go over a few things about the Bulldogs' offensive game plan…then receivers coach Williams pores over the playbook with the two-way star…secondary coach Matthews needs a little bit of Bailey's time…then ESPN needs a word…CBS and CNN…" and so on.

Whether it was tackling, pass defense, intercepting, receiving, rushing, or returning a punt, Bailey could've been considered a sextuple threat —*That's dirty*! He won the Bronko Nagurski Trophy in 1998 as the best defensive player in the nation. Also, he finished seventh in the Heisman Trophy votes in 1998 against names like Daunte Culpepper, Donovan McNabb, and Ricky Williams (the winner).

Champ had an outstanding career in the NFL with the Washington Redskins and the Denver Broncos. He was the seventh overall pick in the 1999 draft.

David Greene

"I don't think people realize how many different highs and lows you go through in a season. It's like a rollercoaster ride because every day is different."

David Greene is one of those players who achieved glory in college, but never played a game in the NFL. He was the starting quarterback for the Bulldogs from 2001 to 2004. He set numerous UGA passing records and his career 11,528 passing yards is an SEC record.

Greene started out as a red shirt freshman and led the Dawgs to their first SEC championship in twenty years. With his passing skills, he became the SEC Rookie of the Year and was named Player of the Year in 2002. He broke Peyton Manning's record for most career wins, with 42. (The record was later broken again.)

- 2001 SEC Offensive Rookie of the Year
- 2002 SEC Offensive Player of the Year
- SEC Record for Pass Attempts without an Interception – 214

Attempts	Completions	Yards	TDs	Rating
1440	849	11528	72	138.3

Garrison Hearst

Garrison Hearst came onto the UGA gridiron after tearing it up with the Lincoln County Red Devils in 1989. Even though his first two years with Georgia were noteworthy, his junior year put him in the running for the Heisman Trophy. He totaled more than 1,500 rushing yards and 21 touchdowns, which led the nation. Nineteen of those touchdowns were from rushing, which was an SEC single-season record. Against Vanderbilt in 1992, he rushed for 246 yards. Hearst also had the second highest total rushing yards in UGA history, behind the invincible Herschel Walker. He was SEC Player of the Year, and came in third place in the Heisman vote tally.

There were many comparisons to Herschel Walker in Hearst's junior year. The fact that he didn't carry the ball much his first two seasons made some wonder if he could have competed with some of Walker's records. UGA's school newspaper, the *Red and Black*, wrote in 1992: "Hearst not only had to fight for playing time with Ware, but also Eric Zeier and Georgia's new pass-oriented offense. As a result, he ran only 153 times."

Hearst was the third pick of the draft by the Arizona Cardinals. In 1995 he was the Comeback Player of the Year, totaling 1,070 rushing yards. He earned the same honors in 2001, when he made a comeback after being out for two years. Hearst had four seasons in the NFL with over 1,000 rushing yards, and in 1998 he rushed for 1,570 yards.

- SEC record for 19 rushing touchdowns in a season
- SEC record for average gain per rush at 6.79 yards (min. 200 attempts)
- NFL Comeback Player of the Year twice

Rushing Attempts	Rushing Yards	Rushing Average	Touchdowns
543	3232	6.0	33

Terry Hoage

You may know Terry Hoage from his vineyards, but before wine he dabbled a little in a game called football. Hoage joined the Bulldogs in 1980 and played defensive back until 1983. He was All-American in 1982 and 1983. In 1982 he set an SEC record by snagging twelve interceptions in a season. Hoage is also tied with two others for the most interceptions in a game at UGA: three.

Terry played thirteen seasons in the NFL as a safety. He was drafted by the New Orleans Saints in 1984, the sixty-eighth pick in the third round. His defensive skills allowed him to play for the Eagles, Redskins, 49ers, Oilers, and finish his career with the Cardinals. After he retired he bought a vineyard, and his wine has received top honors. Many of the names of his wines toy with football in some manner; the Hedge was named for the famous Hedges at Sanford Stadium.

Knowshon Moreno

Born in New Jersey on July 16, 1987, Knowson Moreno made his way to the University of Georgia in 2006. He started as a red shirt freshman in 2007 and received the SEC Freshman of the Year award. Twice he received First-Team All-SEC honors and was Georgia's offensive MVP. Knowshon's acrobatics were clearly defined after he actually hurdled over Central Michigan defender Vince Agnew in his sophomore season.

In 2009, Moreno was the twelfth pick in the draft by the Denver Broncos. Off to a great start, he rushed for 947 yards, and scored seven touchdowns in his rookie season. His playing time and stats hit a downward spiral in the next couple of years. In 2012, he seemed to move in the right direction and almost tripled his rushing yards from 2011, and he only played in eight games.

Moreno was benched after fumbling the ball early in 2012, but no one saw him complaining. When he finally received the chance to play again, he showed up his critics. He was the AFC offensive player of the week in mid-December, and teammate Peyton Manning said, "It's awesome. The team was fired up. It's a great lesson about being a professional."

Rushing Attempts	Rushing Yards	Rushing Average	Touchdowns
498	2734	5.5	30

David Pollack

"My first observation is David Pollack is a warrior," said Mark Richt. "He has the heart of a lion."

David Pollack was one of the best defensive players for UGA, and many considered him to be an unstoppable force. He started out at Shiloh High School, where he was a football, wrestling, and basketball star. When he attended UGA in 2001, he made a name for himself right from the start. His final three years were even better, considering that he was First-Team All-SEC and First-Team All-American from 2002 to 2004.

Pollack received the Chuck Bednarik Award for best defensive player of the year, according to the Maxwell Football Club, in 2004. He won the first Lott Trophy for performance and character and the

Rotary Lombardi Award for the best college linebacker of the year in 2004. In both his junior and senior years, he won the Ted Hendricks Award for the best defensive end in college football.

David Pollack was the seventeenth overall NFL draft pick by the Cincinnati Bengals in 2005. In the second game of his second season he broke his sixth vertebrae when he tackled the Brown's running back. It was a career-ending injury. After he retired, he went on to work for ESPN as an analyst and commentator.

- Held Georgia record for QB sacks in a season: 14
- Holds Georgia record for QB sacks all-time: 36
- SEC Player of the Year: 2002 and 2004

Tackles	Sacks	Interceptions	Touchdowns
283	36	4	1

Jake Scott

"…the most gifted all-around athlete combined with the love and determination to play the game was Jake Scott."

Jake Scott was born in South Carolina, in 1945, but he grew up in Athens. When he attended college at UGA he became an exceptional safety and punt returner. He holds the Georgia records for career interceptions, with sixteen, and interception return yards, with 315. Even Vince Dooley believed Scott was the best all-around player he'd seen.

Scott had a stellar career for the Miami Dolphins from 1970 to 1975 and the Washington Redskins from 1976 to 1978. He was selected to the Pro Bowl in 1971, 1972, 1973, 1974, and 1975, and was the Super Bowl Most Valuable Player in 1973. He was inducted in the Georgia Sports Hall of Fame and the College Football Hall of Fame.

Punt Return Yards	Interceptions	Interception Return Yards
586	16	315

Frank Sinkwich

"I'm from Ohio, but if I'd known when I was two what it was like down South, I would have crawled here on my hands and knees."

Frank Sinkwich's parents were born in Georgia before they emigrated ...to Georgia. *Huh?* His folks were from the country of Georgia. *Oh I get it.* After being signed by the Bulldogs and playing for their freshman team, he made All-American in 1941. He won the Heisman in 1942 with 1,059 votes; the next closest player had 218 votes.

In 1943 he was drafted by the Detroit Lions and played two superb seasons, before the unthinkable happened. He received a career ending knee injury while playing football for the Air Force. After he retired, he held a few coaching positions before beginning a successful career as a beer distributor in Athens, Georgia. *Beer and Athens don't go together at all...* The *Red and Black* wrote on November 27, 1942:

> ...Frankie is more than just All-America. He made Georgia click for four seasons. He has been the spark that set the Bulldogs on fire. Sinkwich is Georgia! Beyond a shadow of a doubt, the Fireball is one of football's all-time greats.

No one will ever wear his number, 21, for the Georgia Bulldog football team again.

He wore a precursor to the face mask due to a broken jaw.

He once played with sprained ankles

Rushing Attempts	Rushing Yards	Rushing Average	TDs
447	2271	5.1	28

Matthew Stafford

Football analyst Mel Kiper Jr. said on ESPN Radio, "Matthew Stafford eventually will be the number one pick in the NFL draft. Write that down." A die hard Georgia fan, David A. Werner said practically the same thing, "Just you wait, boy, he's gonna be number one in that there draft, sure as prayin' on Sunday." They were both right!

In 2006 Matthew Stafford received UGA's Offensive Newcomer of the Year Award and was named to the SEC Coaches' All-Freshman Team. He was All-American in 2008 and named second-team All-SEC in 2008.

Stafford is third all-time at Georgia in pass attempts with 987, and he could have been first if he'd played one more year like those ranked one and two. He is also tied with Aaron Murray, Joe Cox, D.J. Shockley and David Greene for the most touchdown passes in a game: five.

After being drafted by the Detroit Lions, he beat Daunte Culpepper for the starting job in 2009. In 2011, Stafford became the fourth quarterback in NFL history to reach 5000 passing yards in a season. Whereas he didn't break many records in college, he has been on a tear in the NFL.

- Youngest player to throw 5 or more touchdowns in a game
- Most consecutive games with more than 350 passing yards: 4
- Franchise record for most passing yards in a game: 520

Attempts	Completions	Yards	TDs	Rating
987	564	7731	51	133.3

Bill Stanfill

Bill Stanfill was born in Cairo, Georgia, on January 13, 1947. He participated in high school football, basketball, and track and field. Using what he learned in his younger days, he played defensive tackle for the Georgia Bulldogs from 1966 to 1968. He was All-SEC from 1966 to 1968, winning the Outland Trophy for best interior lineman in 1968. Vince Dooley once said, "He was the best defensive lineman we ever had here at Georgia."

He joined the Miami Dolphins in 1969 and made First Team All-Pro in 1972 and 1973. He retired in 1976 and went on to live in Albany, Georgia, as a real estate broker. He's member of the Georgia Sports Hall of Fame and the College Football Hall of Fame.

Fran Tarkenton

The Virginia native Fran Tarkenton blew up the scene in Athens even before attending UGA, leading his high school, the Athens Trojans, to the state championships. He led the Bulldogs to the SEC championships in 1959, while setting an SEC record for pass completion percentage. As captain of the Bulldogs, Tarkenton was named an All-American in 1960.

He was the twenty-ninth draft pick in 1961 and had a record shattering career in the NFL. Tarkenton led the Minnesota Vikings to the Super Bowl three times and was Player of the Year in 1975. It didn't take long for him to be inducted into the Georgia Sports Hall of Fame.

Nine Pro Bowl Selections
Three Super Bowl rings

Attempts	Completions	Yards	TDs	Rating
317	186	2100	18	120.4

Charley Trippi

Part of the toughest generation (World War II generation), Charley Trippi was born in the coal country of Pennsylvania in 1920. He started with the Georgia varsity team in 1942 and played halfback, after Frank Sinkwich was moved to fullback. With his running ability, he helped lead the Bulldogs to SEC championship wins in 1942 and 1946.

Trippi was signed by the Chicago Cardinals and played for nine seasons at quarterback, halfback, punter, and part of the defense. After his football career, he was a coach for the Cardinals and then coached baseball for the University of Georgia. As of this writing, he still resides in Athens. His number 62 is one of only four numbers to be retired at UGA.

It is a rare occurrence for a rival team to say something nice about a player, but Mildred Carpenter of the *Technique* (Georgia Tech's student newspaper) wrote in 1947 when Trippi briefly played for the Crackers: "We have denounced Mr. Trippi and his football team for years, so with his arrival in our midst in a baseball uniform, it will be a welcome change to say nice things about him. For we definitely recognize Trippi's football prowess - he has left no doubt in Tech minds as to that fact..."

🏈 **Played briefly for the Atlanta Crackers baseball team**

🏈 **Member of the Georgia Sports and Pro Football Hall of Fame**

🏈 **Once wore basketball shoes for better traction on an icy Chicago field**

Rushing Attempts	Rushing Yards	Rushing Average	Touchdowns
278	1737	6.2	31

Herschel Walker

"I designed some great plays while Herschel was there that never worked again after he left," Vince Dooley once said of Herschel Walker.

The three-time All-American running back from Wrightsville, Georgia, wasn't the stellar athlete in high school...oh wait, yeah, he was... 3,167 rushing yards his senior year isn't too shabby. He showed no hesitation in his first year at UGA, accumulating 1,616 rushing yards, which is third on the school's records list. The funny part about that is that Walker holds the first and second place records too. He was third in the Heisman Trophy voting for 1980, second in 1981, and finally won the coveted trophy in 1982.

Walker holds SEC records for most rushes in a season (385), most rushes in a career (994), single season rushing yards (1891), most rushing touchdowns in a career (49), and more. But to write three pages about Herschel Walker's records is over doing it.

After his college days, Walker played three seasons of professional football for the New Jersey Generals in the short-lived United States Football League. He rushed for more than 1,800 yards and scored seventeen touchdowns in his first season with the Generals. Walker signed with the NFL's Dallas Cowboys in 1986. He rushed for more than 3,300 yards in four seasons with the Cowboys. He was later traded to the Minnesota Vikings for five players and six draft picks, which was unheard of at the time.

His career never again reached the high note of his third NFL season. He later played for the Eagles and the Giants, and he ended his NFL career where it started, in Dallas. In recent years, Walker has been involved in mixed martial arts and his record was 2-0 in 2013. *This guy is a robot!*

- Participant in the 1992 Winter Olympics in the tandem bobsled competition and placed seventh
- Does more than 2,500 sit-ups and 1,000 pushups daily since high school

Rush Att	Rush Yard	Rush Ave	TDs
994	5259	5.3	49

Notables

Graham Batchelor

Batchelor became a special type of talent, big and fast. Something of a sports renaissance man, he played football, boxed, and was a SEC title-winning track-and-field wonder. He played center for the Bulldogs and was an All-SEC selection in 1933. For some reason it took more than sixty years, until 1996, for Batchelor to be inducted into the Georgia Sports Hall of Fame.

Buck Belue

Everyone can name the running back who led the Bulldogs to the 1980 National Championship game. *Herschel something, right?* What about the quarterback? Often overshadowed is the "man with a plan," Buck Belue. He played four years for Georgia (1978-1981) and the team had a 37-9-1 record in those years. Belue was also an amazing baseball player who started all four years at UGA then played several years in the Expos organization. Today, he can be heard on 680 the Fan as part of the Buck and Kincade radio show. The Georgia Sports Hall of Fame inducted him in 2013.

John Bond

Bond...John Bond. He was a back and punter, totaling more than one thousand yards during his years at Georgia in the 1930s. Besides his running capability, he could also punt the heck out of the ball. Back when the players held multiple positions, Bond averaged more than 40 yards a punt and 4.3 yards per carry. In 1935, he was an All-American and captain of the Dawgs.

Zeke Bratkowski

Known for his NFL career, Bratkowski played quarterback with the Green Bay Packers and helped them win the first two Super Bowls in 1966 and 1967. He was All-SEC in 1953, playing for the Bulldogs, and set a record for passing yards (4863). Bratkowski was the seventeenth selection in the 1953 NFL draft and later became part of the UGA Circle of Honor. *There won't be any Polish jokes for this guy...*

John Carson

Here's Johnny! ...on the golf course, the baseball diamond, the basketball court and, of course, on the gridiron. Lettering in four sports seems unimaginable these days. John Carson caught forty-five passes in 1953, setting a UGA record. His grandfather was a famous Georgian, "Fiddlin" John Carson, one of the first stars of country bluegrass music. The younger Carson played pro football for the Redskins and later scouted for other pro teams. He is in UGA's Circle of Honor and the Georgia Sports Hall of Fame.

Edgar Chandler Jr.

Chandler was an offensive guard for UGA and helped lead the team to the Cotton Bowl in 1967. Before Georgia, he was part of another Bulldog's team in Cedartown, led by legendary coach Doc Ayers. An All-American in 1966 and 1967, he later played in the AFL and NFL with teams such as the Buffalo Bills and the New England Patriots. Unfortunately, he died from cancer at the young age of 46.

Knox Culpepper

In the early 1980s, Knox Culpepper was the defense for Georgia. He still holds several Georgia records, like total tackles in a game (26 against Georgia Tech). Culpepper is first and second in total tackles in a season, with 176 and 170. In the mid-1980s, Canada called and asked him to join the Calgary Stampeders; he accepted the invitation.

Van Andrew Davis

Van Davis was a member of the early 1940s Bulldogs team that won the SEC championship in 1942. He caught thirty-three passes during the 1942 season, leading the conference. In other sports, he could also crush a baseball and was known for his homerun prowess in the Georgia State League. Later, he was drafted by the Green Bay Packers and also played for the All-America Football Conference's New York Yankees. Davis was inducted into the Georgia Sports Hall of Fame in 1994.

Terrence Edwards

Terrence Edwards holds the SEC record for career receiving yards and is second on the all-time SEC list for career receiving touchdowns. He signed with the Atlanta Falcons, playing one season (and catching only one pass), and then he went to the Canadian League. Finally, he found professional success as a wide receiver for the Montreal Alouettes (as in the French children's song, which is about a boy killing a lark for waking him) and the Winnipeg Blue Bombers.

Joe Geri

Joe Geri is another player from that generation that could do everything: pass, catch, run and kick. He played for Georgia in 1942, 1946, 1947, and 1948 helping them to an 84 percent winning percentage while he was on the team. His point-after conversion percentage was an SEC record and he also played in four bowl games. After college he played for the Pittsburgh Steelers and the Chicago Cardinals in the NFL.

Todd Gurley

As of this writing Todd Gurley played one season of college football. In his freshman year he passed Knowshon Moreno for sixth place in rushing yards for a season at Georgia. He is also in second place in the Georgia record books with an average gain per rush of 6.2 yards (minimum 200 attempts). The young running back is in second place, only behind Herschel Walker, for most rushing yards in a season for a freshman, with 1,385. This guy is going places...

Rodney Hampton

Rodney Hampton was Georgia's star running back in the late 1980s. He still holds the UGA record for average gain per rush in a season, with 7.06 in his freshman year. Hampton went on to play his entire NFL career with the New York Giants and had five seasons with more than 1,000 rushing yards. He retired in 1997 at the young age of 28.

William C. Hartman

Bill Hartman was a fullback and linebacker who could also punt a football over them mountains... An All-American in 1937, he set a Bulldog record of fourteen punts in a game. After his playing days, he coached under Wall Butts for eighteen years and then under Ray Goff in the 1990s. He was inducted into the Georgia Sports Hall of Fame in 1981 and the UGA Circle of Honor in 1999.

Andy Johnson

Andy Johnson was born in 1953 in Athens, Georgia, and lettered in football and baseball. He started off as a quarterback, but switched to running back when he turned pro. At Georgia he had twenty-one touchdowns from rushing and nine more from passing. Johnson had over 3,300 total yards from 1971 to 1973 and was drafted by the New England Patriots, playing off and on from 1974 to 1982.

Jarvis Jones

Jarvis Jones started out with the University of Southern California, but after a neck injury, he asked for his release and transferred to Georgia. In 2011 he was First-Team All-American and led the SEC in sacks with 13. In the 2012 season, Jones broke the UGA single-season sacks record set by David Pollack in 2002. Jones tops the list with 14.5. In April 2013, Jones was drafted by Pittsburgh as the seventeenth overall pick.

Guy McIntyre

Guy McIntyre was a guard from Thomasville and an All-SEC selection in 1982 and 1983. He played alongside Herschel Walker in the 1980 National Championship. After college he played in the NFL for the 49ers, Packers, and the Eagles. The five-time Pro-Bowl selection and three-time All-Pro was inducted into the Georgia Sports Hall of Fame in 2007.

Aaron Murray

Aaron Murray passed Peyton Manning for the number two spot on the SEC passing touchdown record list. He holds the UGA record for passing yards in a season (3,893) and holds the school record for passing efficiency rating in a season (174.8). The Georgia gridiron will see Murray for one more year in 2013, as he decided to stay for his senior year.

George E. Patton

Not to be confused with General George S. Patton, but it's probable that he knocked over a German or two on the field. The defensive tackle was an All-American in 1965 and 1966. After college, he played one year with the Atlanta Falcons. He was inducted into the Georgia Sports Hall of fame in 1991 and is a member of UGA's Circle of Honor.

George Poschner

There should be some other award given to the athletes who also fought in wars. George Poschner was an All-American in 1942 and All-SEC in 1941. After his 1942 season he went to war and earned the Bronze Star and Distinguished Service Cross (second-highest medal). This magnificent hero lost his legs due to machine gun fire during the Battle of the Bulge. He was inducted into the Georgia Sports Hall of Fame in 1982.

Theron Sapp

Theron Sapp is one of only four former UGA players to have their jersey numbers retired (the others are Herschel Walker, Frank Sinkwich, and Charley Trippi). His nickname "the Droughtbreaker" was given after he scored the only points of the game against Georgia Tech in 1957, when Tech had beaten Georgia in their eight previous meetings. He played professionally for the Philadelphia Eagles and the Pittsburgh Steelers.

James Skipworth Jr.

Again, the ball-player-soldier award is needed. James Skipworth was voted captain by the 1939 lettermen of the UGA team and played for two years in the late 1930s and early 1940s. The native of Columbus, Georgia, later died for his country in World War II. He was awarded the Silver Star for gallantry during the recapture of the Philippines. In 1960, he was inducted into the Georgia Sports Hall of Fame.

Royce Smith

Royce Smith was born in 1949 in Savannah, Georgia. He was an All-American in 1971 and All-SEC in 1970 and 1971 as an offensive guard. In 1972, the New Orleans Saints snatched him as the eighth pick in the NFL draft. From 1975 to 1976 he played closer to home with the Atlanta Falcons. Smith was inducted into the Georgia Sports Hall of Fame in 1995 and sadly, he passed away at the age of 54 in 2004.

Vernon Smith

Vernon "Catfish" Smith was a three-sport star (basketball, baseball, and football) for the University of Georgia. Supposedly, he earned that nickname as a kid by biting off the head of a fish in a bet. He was All-American in 1931. His most memorable moment came in a game against Yale, thought to be the better team. Smith scored every point for Georgia. He tackled for a safety, caught a pass in the end zone, kicked an extra point, and blocked a punt in the end zone. The Bulldogs won!

Bobby Walden

Bobby Walden could kick a ball well enough to lead the NCAA with an average of forty-three yards per punt in 1958. He was nicknamed "the Big Toe from Cairo" and once punted the ball seventy-eight yards against the Citadel. The All-SEC selection played professionally after college, first in the Canadian Football League and then for fourteen years in the NFL. He played for such teams as the Edmonton Eskimos, Hamilton Tiger-Cats, Minnesota Vikings, and the Pittsburgh Steelers.

Hines Ward

Former UGA offensive player Hines Ward set numerous records for the Pittsburgh Steelers in the NFL. His versatility at Georgia allowed him to play multiple positions, including wide receiver, tailback, and quarterback. He also won the 2011 season of *Dancing with the Stars*.

James 'Big Jim' Wilson

Big Jim was inducted into the Georgia Sports Hall of Fame in 2001. Born in 1942, he became an offensive tackle and an All-American. After college he played in the NFL for the 49ers, the Falcons, and the Rams. He only played for a few years and had to retire due to an injury to his spine. Big Jim found a new calling in life in the form of professional wrestling. He passed away from cancer at the age of 67 in 2009.

George 'Kid' Woodruff

George "Kid" Woodruff was one of the first stars of Georgia football. He played quarterback during his tenure and was the team captain in 1911. Although he graduated in 1912, he didn't play that year due to his parents' fears about the dangers of football. He held the rank of major in World War I and when he returned he ran an insurance business. In 1923, Woodruff became the coach of Georgia's football team, earning the salary of one dollar a year. After seven years as head coach his record was 30-16-1. ...and if it weren't for his insurance business, he would have been quite broke.

Ben Zambiasi

Most people know Ben Zambiasi from the Hamilton Tiger-Cats. *Huh? Maybe if you're Canadian...* Zambiasi is the Georgia record holder for total tackles in a career: 467. He played football in the Canadian League and is in the league's hall of fame.

Eric Zeier

Eric Zeier was named First-Team All-American in 1994. He set more than sixty Bulldog records and eighteen SEC records. He still holds the UGA records for pass completions in a season (269), passing yards in a game (top 3 slots), and is second in passing yards in a season (3525).

In 1956, UGA I was dog-napped by fraternity brothers from the University of North Carolina, but returned home safely.

Coaches

Glenn Scobey 'Pop' Warner

The University of Georgia's football program started in 1892, and in 1895 the school added a new coach to the team. Glenn Scobey "Pop" Warner, who once said, "You play the way you practice," played football for Cornell. He was the oldest player on the team and was crowned Pop by his teammates. His many adjustments to the game have stood the test of time. Here are a few:

- **Spiral Punt**: A punt in which the ball spins on its axis and goes far …real far.
- **Naked Bootleg**: The quarterback runs toward the sideline behind the line of scrimmage without a blocker, usually after a fake hand-off to the running back.
- **Double Reverse**: When a quarterback runs toward the sideline, hands off to a wide receiver, who then runs the opposite direction, and hands off to another player.
- **Single Wing Formation**: A tight-end and a receiver align together and the ball is snapped (not handed). This laid the foundation for the shotgun formation.
- **Double Wing Formation**: Any offensive formation with two wingbacks.
- **Screen Pass**: A trick play intended to fool the defense into thinking it will be a long pass, when, in actuality, it is a short pass.

Warner's coaching record for UGA was 7-4, with a 3-4 first season and an undefeated second. He was a major advocate of the spiral pass, when most people were not fans of throwing the ball. Warner went on to coach at the Carlisle Indian School, where the legendary Jim Thorpe played. He led four teams to national championships. In his coaching career he compiled a record 319-106-32.

W.A. Cunningham

W. A. Cunningham was the Georgia coach who took his leadership abilities from the gridiron to the fields of war, becoming a general in the U.S. Army. A graduate of Vanderbilt University in Nashville, Tennessee, he was the first Georgia coach to stay for more than three seasons. Not only that, but Cunningham had originally coached the Gordon Prep School baseball team, which beat UGA 10-0. UGA's athletics director S. V. Sanford, negotiated a contract with the coach right after that game. In eight seasons with UGA he had only one losing season.

In 1910, the *Athens Weekly Banner* reported that "Coach W.A. Cunningham has taken a bunch of green men, rather lighter than the average material in the south this past season, and molded them into a fast, gritty and thoroughly well-coached machine that made a record which entitles the eleven to be recognized as one of the best in Georgia's history."

As the United States entered the Great War, the Banner's Carey J. Williams wrote that, "Coach Cunningham forsook the football field for the battlefield, and won a commission in the army as a major. He was awarded the D.S.C. (Distinguished Service Cross) for his gallant services on the battlefield..." Cunningham left UGA with a record of 43-18-9 and made the U.S. safer by putting his talents into the armed forces.

Wally Butts

Besides having the best name ever, Wally Butts was also a remarkable football player and coach. "I don't care where a man comes from or how he spells his name. All I ask is that he be loyal to Georgia, proud of that jersey and try like the devil to win."

Butts attended college at Mercer University, where he played a little gridiron football. When he took on the coaching job at UGA in 1939, he took the Georgia team to a national championship...twice. The first one would come in 1942 (consensus) and the second would come in 1946 (one poll). He coached some of the best talents to ever set foot on the field. The Heisman Trophy winner, Frank Sinkwich helped Georgia secure the National Championship in 1942, while Charley Trippi helped in 1946. There could have easily been another championship if it hadn't been for the war.

Butts compiled a record of 140-86-9, the highest number of wins for a Georgia coach at the time. In 1966 he made it to the Georgia Sports Hall of Fame and was inducted into the College Football Hall of Fame in 1997. He was also the SEC Coach of the Year in 1942, 1946, and 1959.

Vince Dooley

...And then God created Vince Dooley. He is best known for dominating Florida and Georgia Tech, two of the Bulldogs' all-time rivals. Under Dooley's leadership, a teenage Herschel Walker swept into UGA and helped the team go big. Dooley coached the Bulldogs for twenty-five years and set a UGA record of 201 wins. He was only thirty-one when Georgia hired him, but he brought the Dawgs to a 7-3-1 record like a seasoned veteran. Dooley's worst year came in 1977, when the Bulldogs dipped below the .500 mark, the only time in his Georgia career that happened.

Dooley was born in Mobile, Alabama on September 4, 1932. He attended Auburn University where he played basketball and football. After graduating, he entered the Marine Corps for two years, and then he held various coaching positions at Auburn.

In 1963, Dooley was hired by the Georgia Bulldogs as their head coach. He would go on to lead Georgia to six SEC championship wins. In 1979, he became the UGA athletic director, a position he held until 2003. Dooley is in the Georgia Circle of Honor, the College Football Hall of Fame, the Georgia Sports Hall of Fame, the Alabama Sports Hall of Fame, and was SEC Coach of the Year seven times.

Mark Richt

Although born in Omaha on February 18, 1960, Mark Richt grew up in Boca Raton, the northern retiree's Mecca. He started as a back-up quarterback to Jim "Machine Gun" Kelly at the University of Miami then became quarterback's coach for fourteen seasons at FSU. While at FSU, Richt was the offensive coordinator for seven years before making the move to UGA for the head coaching position.

In his first year as the Bulldog's coach, the team's record was 8-4. It had been eighty years since a Georgia coach reached the eight-win mark in their first year. Year two brought about the school's first SEC championship since 1982. After the Bulldogs won the SEC championship in 2005, he was selected as the SEC Coach of the Year.

Richt has six SEC Eastern Division titles under his belt and boasts a record of 118-40, as of 2012. He is a two-time SEC Coach of the Year and has an 8-4 bowl record.

Must Mentions

Larry Munson

Larry Munson made his way down from Minnesota to take over as one of the Braves announcers when the team came to Atlanta. After that brief stint, he moved to Athens to do the radio play-by-play from 1966 to 2008. He became, without a doubt, the voice of the Bulldogs. His distinct voice and on-air vernacular were amusing and exciting. Objectivity was not his forte; he announced play-by-play, as a fan, as these examples illustrate:

> Hunker down, you guys! If you didn't hear me, you guys, hunker down! I know I'm asking a lot, you guys, but hunker it down one more time! *–From the 1982 Auburn game that secured the SEC title for Georgia*

> We hand it off to Herschel, there's a hole...5..10..12, he's running over people! Oh, you Herschel Walker! My God Almighty, he ran right through two men! Herschel ran right over two men! They had him dead away inside the 9. Herschel Walker went 16 yards. He drove right over those orange shirts and is just driving and running with those big thighs. My God, a freshman! *–From Herschel Walker's first touchdown*

> Touchdown! My God, a touchdown! We threw it to Haynes with 5 seconds left! My God almighty, did you see what we did?! We just stomped on their face with a hob-nailed boot and broke their nose!! *–From a 2001 game against Tennessee for the win*

Munson was inducted to the Georgia Sports Hall of Fame in 2005.

Dan Magill

Dan Magill is to the Georgia Bulldogs as the color orange is to oranges. *Worst. Analogy. Ever...* Magill grew up in Athens and started with the Bulldogs as a batboy for the baseball team in the early 1930s. After he graduated from UGA with a degree in journalism, he wrote for the *Atlanta Journal* in the sports department. After he became the sports information director for the Bulldogs, he created the *Georgia Bulldog Newspaper* to help promote the team during a time when they were in the doldrums. In an article, David Ching wrote, "At football coach Wally Butts' behest, Magill crossed the back roads throughout the state in a red and black station wagon, installing a Georgia Bulldog Club in every Georgia county over three summers in the 1950s."

In the 1950s, Magill became the head coach for Georgia's tennis program. After thirty-years, he compiled a record of 706-183, which is second place in the NCAA record book. Also, he selected UGA I as the first of a long line of bulldog mascots for Georgia in 1956. Magill became a member of the Georgia Sports Hall of Fame in 1976.

Georgia Tech Football

Following in the footsteps of UGA, the Georgia School of Technology started up their football program in 1892, after watching UGA lose to Auburn in Atlanta 10-0. Their first football coach had much in common with the first coach up in Athens: both men were science professors. Tech's first coach was Ernest E. West, a professor of physics and also the captain of the team. Their first season was more than upsetting; they were 0-3, losing to Mercer, Vanderbilt, and Auburn.

The next season brought Tech a little more hope in the form of their new coach and captain, Medal of Honor recipient Leonard Wood. He fought in the Spanish-American War, the Philippine-American War, and helped in the campaign to capture Geronimo. He was the Republican nominee for president in 1920. He lost the election, but his first game with Tech was a pretty good beating of Georgia, 28-6. Overall, the first twelve years for Georgia Tech football weren't kind; the team's record from 1892 to 1903 was 9-32-5.

John Heisman became Georgia Tech's coach in 1904, and with Johnny at the helm, the team was about to change forever. Heisman led Tech to an 8-1-1 season and held a Tech record of 102-29-7. In 1916, Tech beat Cumberland College 220-0. Cumberland had recently dismantled its football program, so the players had little football experience. Nevertheless, it was a slaughter.

The following year was a good one for Heisman and the Yellow Jackets. With the help of Everett Strupper, Tech went 9-0 and became national champions. The opposing teams scored a total of 17 points, while Tech averaged more than 54 points per game. Heisman moved from Atlanta after separating with his wife and agreeing not to live in the same city. Tech lost one of the best coaches of all time. In 1936, the Downtown Athletic Club named its award for the best college football player of the year in his honor, the John W. Heisman Memorial Trophy. Georgia Tech players, however, have yet to win the Heisman.

After Heisman left, assistant coach William Alexander took the reins of the Yellow Jacket football team. This was the team that played during the Roaring Twenties, the Great Depression, and World War II. With a little help from players with nicknames like

Father, Shorty, Dutch, and Stumpy, the team won its second national championship by defeating California 8-7 in the 1929 Rose Bowl.

After the game the team was given a bear named Bruin, which became known as "Stumpy's bear" because Stumpy Thomason took care of it. The bear became a fixture at games and around campus, sleeping under the bleachers at Grant Field.

The 1940s saw the bright star of Clint Castleberry rise and fall as a freshman in contention for the Heisman Trophy. He was third in voting for the Heisman, but played only one year. He was killed in World War II. Not long after, Alexander retired in 1944 with a 134-95-15 record.

Bobby Dodd became coach in 1945 and got off to a rough start with a 4-6 record. Fortunately for Tech, there weren't many losing seasons the next 22 years under Dodd. In fact, under his leadership, the Yellow Jackets had twenty winning seasons. In 1952, Tech claimed the national title, although in most polls Michigan was the national champion. Tech left the SEC in 1963 and became an independent school, like Notre Dame. Dodd retired with a Tech record of 165-64-8 in 1966, staying on as the athletic director.

Bud Carson took over as the new coach in 1967, and had a troubled start; Tech had three-straight losing seasons. Bill Fulcher, Pepper Rodgers, and Bill Curry followed Carson but couldn't bring Tech back to its glory days. Curry coached a winning season and many thought that he was rebuilding, but Alabama eventually lured him away.

With a little help from Coach Bobby Ross, star quarterback Shawn Jones, and running back William Bell, Tech was considered the National Champions by the UPI poll. Soon after this remarkable feat, the Yellow Jackets apparently weren't eating their Wheaties and fell behind in the standings for several years. The former defensive coordinator George O'Leary became head coach and had the team in the green after one season, winning the conference title in 1998, with a record of 10-2. His record by 2001 was 52-33 when he left Tech to join Notre Dame. Because of a few "mix ups" on his resume, he joined UCF instead.

There was a bit of controversy dealing with ineligible players in the late 1990s and early 2000s, and with the hiring and eventual firing of Chan Gailey, Tech was finally on the way back to glory. The school hired Paul Johnson at the end of 2007 and he led the Yellow

Jackets to five bowl games. Tech's record from 2008 to 2012 was 41-26.

Team Highlights

Atlanta, Georgia

First Season: 1892

Conference: Atlantic Coast Conference

Nickname: Yellow Jackets

Colors: White and Gold

Conference Titles: 16

Main Rivals: Georgia, Clemson

No Kiddin'? Once known as the Golden Tornado

Tech's Ramblin' Wreck takes the field during home games. It's a 1930 Ford Model-A Sport Coupe

Legends

Keith Brooking

Keith Brooking was born in Senoia, Georgia, on October 30, 1975. He played for East Coweta High School until 1993, as a tight end and linebacker. A star during those years, he made fifty-three receptions with seven touchdowns and 250 tackles during his time with the Indians.

At Georgia Tech, Brooking was one of the few true freshmen to play in 1994. In his sophomore year he led the ACC with 13.3 hits per game. Over his time with Tech, Brooking had multiple games with 20 tackles, and he became the school's all-time leader in tackles, with 467.

In 1998, he was the twelfth draft pick by the Atlanta Falcons and got off to a fast start his rookie year. In 2001 he was selected to the Pro Bowl, and the following year he reached 200 tackles, a feat accomplished by only five Falcon players.

Brooking played for the Falcons until 2009, when he signed a three-year contract with the Dallas Cowboys. In 2012, he signed a million dollar contract with the Denver Broncos which put him at fifteen years in the NFL.

Kelly Campbell

Born in in Atlanta, in 1980, he began his sporting career at Mays High School and lettered in football, track, and baseball. In his freshmen year he took off rather slowly, totaling eleven receptions and 131 yards. Although he had a slow start, he would go on to be the all-time leader in receptions for Tech, with 195. Also, he holds team records in yards (2907) and touchdowns (24). Campbell ranks third in the ACC for receiving yards and was selected as first-team All-ACC in 1999 and 2001.

After his stellar career in college, he signed with the Minnesota Vikings in 2002, reaching 176 yards and scoring three touchdowns. His best year in the NFL was 2003, when he caught twenty-five passes, putting up 522 reception yards, and scoring four touchdowns. After one more year with the Vikings, he signed with the Dolphins, but due to an injury, he was released. It seems that Campbell found his place in the Canadian Football League with the Edmonton

Eskimos in 2008. He had 1223 receiving yards and scored seven touchdowns.

Receptions	Yards	Rec. TDs	Kick Ret. Yards
195	2907	24	1283

Clint Castleberry

Clint Castleberry was born in 1923, in Atlanta, Georgia, and died somewhere off the coast of Liberia in 1944. Clint Castleberry was a 5 ft. 9 in. half back who played only one season, 1942. He was allowed to play varsity football as a freshman, due to a loss of players during World War II. Due to his unbelievable speed, he once intercepted a pass against Navy and ran for a 95-yard touchdown.

When it came time for Heisman voting, Castleberry came in third place and it was the first time a freshman had even made the ballot. Bulldog Frank Sinkwich ended up winning that year.

Castleberry enlisted in the armed forces and was planning to play again after the war. Unfortunately, this was not to be; a plane that he was co-piloting disappeared off the coast of West Africa in 1944. In December of that year his number 19 was retired as a memorial to Castleberry and all Tech students killed in the war. According to the *Miami Daily News*, "Tech alumni either bought or pledged themselves to buy $4,079,100 in war bonds dedicated to Castleberry as a symbol of all Georgia Tech men who have made the supreme sacrifice."

Joe Guyon

Born in White Earth, Minnesota, on November 26, 1892, Joe Napoleon Guyon was a Chippewa Indian that became an NFL star and an exceptional baseball player. He is not as well-known as another Native American named Jim Thorpe, for he was often cast in his shadow. His abilities as an athlete made him one of the greatest football players to attend Georgia Tech. Guyon made his start at the Carlisle Indian School under former UGA coach, Pop Warner. Several years later, he joined Georgia Tech under Coach John Heisman. He would be a part of the undefeated 1917 National Championship team.

In the Auburn game of 1917, he led the team to a 68-7 victory. According to the *Technique* of December 4, 1917:

> Joe Guyon…played the greatest game of his life. He not only formed strong interference, cutting men down…but ran with the impetus of an interference and runner combined. Auburn could not stop the big Indian, who ran on with would-be tacklers hanging to him. They seemed to have extreme difficulty in catching both legs at once and time after time Joe was seen dragging a tackler who had hold of but one leg.

In the same season, Guyon rushed for 344 yards to help Tech beat Vandy, 83 to nothing.

After college, he turned pro with the Canton Bulldogs in 1919, then played for the Washington Senators, the Union Quakers of Philadelphia, the Cleveland Indians, the Oorang Indians, the Rock Island Independents, the Kansas City Cowboys, and ended with the New York Giants. For several years he played alongside his former Carlisle teammate, Jim Thorpe.

While beginning his professional football career, he must have decided that he didn't have enough on his plate, so he dabbled in professional baseball too. He played for the Augusta Georgians, Little Rock Travelers, the Atlanta Crackers, the Louisville Colonels, and a few other independent teams. Over the course of twelve seasons, he batted .329, with 49 homeruns and 91 triples.

Joe Hamilton

Joe Hamilton was born on March 13, 1977, in Alvin, South Carolina. He played football at Macedonia High School and was a two-time all-state selection. He compiled 5,425 passing yards and 67 touchdowns, and he never threw an interception in his senior year.

He chose Georgia Tech in 1996 and was the runner-up for Rookie of the Year in the ACC. In his sophomore year he was the Jackets MVP and started his streak of breaking Tech records in total offense and completion percentage. Twice he was chosen to the first-team All-ACC and he was consensus All-American in his senior year.

Hamilton is considered one of the best quarterbacks in the history of Georgia Tech. He made his start on an athletic scholarship, and what a start he made. The record books list him as the ACC all-time leader in total yards (10,640), touchdown passes (65), and the highest rating in pass efficiency (148.2). In 1999, Hamilton was second in Heisman Trophy votes, behind Wisconsin's Ron Dayne.

Because of his height (5'10") he was chosen as the 234th pick in the NFL draft by the Tampa Bay Buccaneers. Playing time was limited during his few years in the NFL, so he made the switch to the Arena Football League in 2004. He led the Orlando Predators to the Arena Bowl, but they lost to the Chicago Rush 69-61. As of late, he went on to different coaching positions with Georgia Tech and finally settled with the nascent Georgia State University football program as a running-back coach.

Passing Yards	Passing TDs	Rushing Yards	Rushing TDs	Rating
8882	65	1758	18	148

Eddie Lee Ivery

Eddie Lee Ivery grew up in Thomson, Georgia, just outside of Augusta. Once, while in junior varsity football, he scored four touchdowns in one game. He took an athletic scholarship to Georgia Tech and became one of the best running backs in Tech history under coach Pepper Rodgers. In a 1978 game against Air Force, Ivery rushed for 356 yards, a then NCAA record. On November 15, 1978 the *Press-Courier* reported that "Neither rain, nor a howling 25 mph wind, nor a gnawing stomach ache could deter Georgia Tech's Eddie Lee Ivery from becoming the NCAA's all-time single game rushing leader." Unfortunately, he was eighth in Heisman voting, but he was drafted in the first round by the Green Bay Packers. He was inducted into the Georgia Tech Athletics Hall of Fame in 1983.

Ivery had a tough start in the NFL; he tore his anterior cruciate ligament in his first regular season game. His best year came in 1980 when he rushed for 831 yards and had 50 receptions for 481 yards. In 1982 he injured his knee, ending his season. At this point he began using cocaine and had major troubles off the field. He retired in 1987 and eventually kicked his bad habits. Ivery became a conditioning coach for eight years with Georgia Tech and then moved back to Thomson, Georgia to bring his life lessons to the local high school.

Attempts	Rushing Yards	TDs	Rec. Yards
609	3517	22	406

Calvin Johnson

Calvin Johnson, AKA Megatron, was born on September 29, 1985. He was a first-team All-American selection in 2005 and 2006, and was first-team All-ACC every year of college. In 2006 he was the ACC Player of the Year and won the Fred Biletnikoff Award and the Paul Warfield Trophy for being the top college wide receiver. Johnson holds the Georgia Tech record for reception yards with 2,927.

In 2007, the Detroit Lions picked Johnson as the second overall pick in the NFL draft. With the Lions, he has set franchise records and NFL records in just six seasons. He currently holds the record for receiving yards in a season with 1,964 in 2012, eleven games with 100 or more receiving yards in a season, and eight consecutive games with 100 or more yards. Johnson is also the only player in the NFL to have had more than 1600 reception yards in two consecutive seasons.

Receptions	Yards	TDs
178	2927	28

Kim King

Kimbrough King was the quarterback for Georgia Tech from 1965 to 1967, and is considered one of the best to take the field. He was the last quarterback under the legendary Bobby Dodd, and after his college career he became a savvy businessman and radio announcer for Tech.

King led the Yellow Jackets to two bowl games and ended his career with multiple passing records. After graduation he didn't play any pro football and decided to make it in the business world. He became a successful commercial real estate developer in the Atlanta area and was also the finance chairman for Gov. Roy Barnes.

King started doing color analysis for Tech games in 1974 and kept this gig for three decades. Sadly, he lost his battle with leukemia in October 2004.

He was inducted into the Georgia Tech Sports Hall of Fame in 1978 and the Georgia Sports Hall of Fame in 1996.

Completions	Yards	TDs	Interceptions
243	2763	14	23

Robert Lavette

Robert Lavette was born in September 8, 1963, in Cartersville, Georgia. He may be one of the most underrated running backs in Tech football history. This could be because of being Herschel Walker's shadow for two years, but who knows? The fact remains that he holds many of Tech's rushing records and he just doesn't get the press he should. His freshman and junior years were quality, but his sophomore and senior years were sensational. He was just under 2,400 yards in those two years combined, with thirty-three touchdowns. He also racked up 114 receptions in his four years with the Yellow Jackets.

His 4,066 rushing yards and 5393 total yards are Tech records, as are his forty-six rushing touchdowns. After graduation he was grabbed in the fourth round of the NFL draft by the Dallas Cowboys. He spent three season with the Cowboys working mainly as a kick return specialist, before spending his final year in the pros with the Eagles. Lavette is a member of the Georgia Tech Sports Hall of Fame.

Rushing	R TDs	Rec	Rec.TDs
4066	45	862	1

The Rhinos

When your last name is Rhino the odds are high that you will become one of two things: a football player or a circus sideshow. In this case it's the former, and it's more like a crash of rhinos, because there were not one, but two Tech stars to bear this name.

The first Rhino would be Randy, the three-time, first-team All-American. He was a star defensive back and punt returner who played as a Yellow Jacket from 1971 to 1974. Randy is second on the Georgia Tech records list with fourteen career interceptions and he's in the top 20 with 203 career tackles. For a while, he held the Tech record for punt return yardage, with 749 yards, and in 1972 he returned a 96-yard punt in 1972 against the Gamecocks. Rhino was drafted by the New Orleans Saints but chose to play in the Canadian league for five seasons.

His son Kelley also made a name for himself on the football field for Georgia Tech. At only five feet seven inches tall, Kelley filled his father's big shoes and set some school records himself. He surpassed his father on punt returns and set a school record of 1,135 punt return yards. Also, he is second in the ACC, behind Ledel George. It should also be mentioned that Kelley's grandfather and uncle also played Georgia Tech football, making it quite the dynasty.

Lucius Sanford

Lucius Sanford, the Linebacker out of Milledgeville, Georgia, was crucial to the defense of Georgia Tech from 1974 to 1977. He was a three-time All-South Independent and was first-team All-American in 1977. Also, he led Tech in tackles in his last three years and set a record as a freshman with 124 tackles.

Sanford was picked by the Buffalo Bills in the fourth round of the 1978 draft, and played ten years in the NFL as an outside linebacker. In his rookie year with the Bills, he set a record by blocking two field goals in the same game. After playing more than 100 games in the NFL with the Bills and the Browns, he called it quits in 1988.

Billy Shaw

Billy Shaw was born on December 15, 1938, in Natchez, Mississippi. Part of the offensive line at Georgia Tech, Shaw would go on to make a name for himself with the Buffalo Bills as a guard. In 1961, he was an All-American and named to the College All-Star team as a tackle. Shaw was drafted by the Bills in 1961 and made the American Football League All-Star Team eight times. He stayed in the AFL until his retirement in 1969. Though he never even played one game in the NFL, he was inducted to the NFL Pro Football Hall of Fame in 1999.

Notables

David Irenus Barron

David "Red" Barron was born in Clarkesville, Georgia in 1900 and lettered in three different sports while at Tech. He was an All-American selection in 1921 and 1922. Aside from a stellar career as part of the Golden Tornado, he was also part of the Boston Braves, albeit briefly. Barron once played four games with a broken jaw, managed the Crackers in 1932, and later started the football program in Dacula, Georgia. It should also be mentioned that he killed his wife. He is a member of the Georgia Tech and Georgia Sports Hall of Fame, into which he was inducted in 1977.

Maxie Baughan

Maxie Baughan was Georgia Tech's star linebacker in the late 1950s. He was voted Linebacker of the Year by the SEC and was also the team's captain. Born in Forkland, Alabama in 1939, he entered Georgia Tech's Hall of Fame in 1965 and the Georgia Sports Hall of Fame in 1980. After college, he was drafted by the Philadelphia Eagles and spent eleven years in the NFL, making the Pro Bowl in nine of those years. Cornell hired Baughan as their head coach in 1983, and he spent six seasons in New York.

Tashard Choice

Born in Thomasville, Georgia in 1984, Tashard Choice became a star at Lovejoy High School. His college career started with the Oklahoma Sooners, but he transferred after his freshman year. In his junior year he set rushing records for Tech. He had nine games in which he rushed more than 100 yards. Choice was drafted in the fourth round by the Dallas Cowboys and has since played for the Redskins and the Bills.

Willie Clay

Willie Clay, the cornerback from Pittsburgh, was born on September 5, 1970. He attended Georgia Tech on a scholarship and was part of their 1990 title run. Clay topped Jeff Ford and Randy Rhino in career interceptions with sixteen from 1988 to 1991. After college he had a successful career in the NFL with the Lions, Patriots, and the Saints.

PJ Daniels

Prince Ahadzie (P. J.) Daniels was born in Houston on December 21, 1982. What sets Daniels apart from a lot of the players in this book is that he was a walk-on and had to work his butt off to get the starting job as running back. In his sophomore year he averaged more than 111 yards a game and scored ten touchdowns. He set a bowl record in 2003 by rushing 307 yards in the Humanitarian Bowl against Tulsa. When he finished at Tech, he was drafted by the Baltimore Ravens in fourth round in 2006.

Paul A. Duke

Born in 1924 in DeKalb County, Georgia, he walked onto Grant Field and that was that... After being selected as an All-American and All-SEC, he was a lineman for the New York Yankees football team. He was inducted into the Georgia Sports Hall of Fame in 1993. The November 17, 1946 *Pittsburgh Press* wrote that "Duke...gave a forceful demonstration of his All-America eligibility...he plowed into Len Finley's punt and pounced on it on the Tulane two...clutching the ball almost as soon as he blocked it."

Bill Fincher

Bill Fincher was a two time All-American in 1919 and 1920 as a tackle. He was inducted into the College Football Hall of Fame in 1974 and the Georgia Sports Hall of Fame in 1975. Fincher was an assistant coach for Tech, and also coached for a year at the College of William and Mary with a record of 4-3-1.

Allen "Buck" Flowers

"Buck" Flowers was an All-American in 1918 and 1920 and was captain of the "Ramblin' Wreck" football team. He was inducted into the Georgia Sports Hall of Fame in 1969 and was the first player from Tech to be inducted into the College Football Hall of Fame.

Leon Hardeman

When UGA didn't want Leon Hardeman because of his small stature, he found a home at Georgia Tech and proved that size doesn't matter. *Say whaaaat?!* As for honors, he was a two-time All-American running back and averaged 5.3 yards per carry. He scored twenty-two touchdowns in three years at Tech from 1951 to 1953.

He was one of the best running backs in Tech's history. Hardeman was inducted into the Georgia Sports Hall of Fame in 1988.

Steve Harkey

The half back born in 1948 was part of a 9-3, 1970 season under the Bobby Dodd replacement, Coach Bud Carson. He accumulated 995 total yards and five touchdowns in his Yellow Jacket career. Not only did he marry Miss Atlanta, Suzanne Ripley, he was teammates with Joe Namath on the New York Jets in the early 1970s.

Michael Johnson

One of the best defensive players Georgia Tech has ever seen, Michael Johnson made his start in Dallas County as a star receiver. He excelled at basketball too (at 6'7", why not?). With the Yellow Jackets, he was chosen as a First Team All-American in 2008. He totaled 107 tackles and nineteen sacks in four years with Tech. In 2008, he was picked in the third round of the NFL draft by the Cincinnati Bengals.

Billy Lothridge

Cleveland, Georgia, is home to two important things: Cabbage Patch Kids and Billy Dothridge. Dothridge was the quarterback for Gainesville High School and went on to be starting quarterback for Bobby Dodd's Yellow Jackets in 1961. He came in second in the Heisman voting in his senior year. He was drafted by the Oakland Raiders in the sixth round. While he played for other teams like the Rams and the Dolphins, it was with the Falcons that he spent the longest portion of his career, from 1966 to 1971.

Billy Martin

Billy Martin (not the former baseball manager) was a tight end from Gainesville, Georgia and played for Tech from 1961 to 1963. At 6'6", he was a monster and caught for 777 yards in his college career. He later played professionally for the Bears, Falcons, and the Vikings. Many years later, he was inducted into the Georgia Sports Hall of Fame in 1997.

Jerry Mays

Jerry Mays was born on December 8, 1967, in Augusta, Georgia. His is the all-time leading rusher for Thomson High School, and is the second all-time leading rusher for Georgia Tech. He was inducted into the Georgia Tech Athletics Hall of Fame in 1997.

Eddie McAshan

Eddie McAshan was the first African American quarterback to start not only for Georgia Tech but in the southeast as well. He once threw five touchdowns in a game but also five interceptions. McAshan held the Georgia Tech record for interceptions (51), until 2006.

George A. Morris Jr.

As captain of the 1952 squad that won the national championship against Mississippi and compiled a 12-0 record, George Morris was named All-American and All-SEC. The linebacker was picked up by the San Francisco 49ers in the second round of the 1953 draft. Morris was inducted into the Georgia Sports Hall of Fame in 1981 and became an SEC official after his brief stint in the NFL and his work for RC Cola.

Larry Morris

Born in Decatur, Georgia, in 1933, Morris tackled more than 250 opponents in four years with the Ramblin' Wreck. As a lineman, he was All-American twice and All-SEC four years in a row, from 1951 to 1954. He was the seventh pick in the 1954 draft and played in the NFL for the Rams and Bears before ending his career at home with the Falcons. Morris was inducted into the College Football Hall of Fame and the Georgia Sports Hall of Fame.

Henry R. "Peter" Pund

The Augusta native, born in 1907, was part of the team in which the Golden Tornado narrowly beat the Golden Bears in the 1929 Rose Bowl. He was an All-American in 1928 and All-Southern Conference twice as the center for Georgia Tech. Pund is a member of both the College football Hall of Fame and the Georgia Sports Hall of Fame. Notre Dame coach Knute Rockne said of Pund, "Nobody could stop him. Notre Dame fought like tigers …but this man was a tiger-tamer…20 scoring plays that this man ruined."

L. W. Robert

Another one of those magnificent creatures to letter in several sports, Robert was part of that generation that could do anything. Born in 1889, he found success on the field and then later in business and government. He was president of the Atlanta Crackers, Secretary of the Democratic National Committee, and started his own architectural firm. Salting the UGA wound, he played against Georgia four times, with Tech winning each game.

Daryl Smith

An Albany, Georgia native born on March 14, 1982, Daryl Smith was a star baseball player and football linebacker in high school. His 383 tackles, forty-eight tackles for loss, and fifteen sacks were first among Georgia Tech linebackers. In the 2004 NFL draft, he was the thirty-ninth pick by the Jacksonville Jaguars. As of this writing, he holds the Jaguars record for tackles with almost 700.

Albert Staton

Albert Staton was a star football and basketball player for Tech in the early 1920s. He was the first editor of Tech's alumni magazine and later worked for the Coca-Cola Company. Staton was inducted into the Georgia Sports Hall of Fame in 1964.

Everett Strupper

Everett Strupper was born on July 26, 1896, in Columbus, Georgia. He played under legendary coach John Heisman, and the most notable fact about "Stroop" was that he was deaf. While Stroop played at Tech, the team never lost a game and during the famous game against Cumberland, Stroop scored eight touchdowns. He was an All-American in 1917 but never played his senior year since he went to fight in the Great War. He was inducted into the College Football Hall of Fame in 1972 and the Georgia Sports Hall of Fame in 1974.

Pat Swilling

Pat Swilling was at one point the all-time leader in sacks at Georgia Tech and set the ACC record of seven sacks in a game. He was first team All-American in 1985 and was later inducted to the Georgia Sports Hall of Fame in 2004. After his college days, he made his mark in the NFL by playing for 12 seasons with the Saints, Lions, and Raiders. Surpassing mediocrity, he was Defensive Player of the Year in 1989 and was a Pro Bowl selection five times. In the public sector, he served a term in the Louisiana House of Representatives in 2001.

Johnny G. "Stumpy" Thomason

Another member of the 1928 team to defeat the Golden Bears in the Rose Bowl, Thomason led the way as Tech's running back. After college, he played for several seasons for the Brooklyn Dodgers football team and the Philadelphia Eagles throughout the 1930s. He received a brown bear named Bruin as a gift that became a fixture at the Tech campus.

Phillip Wheeler

Born in Columbus, Georgia in 1984, Phillip Wheeler was a standout football star at Shaw High School, where he accumulated more than 100 tackles. At Tech, the linebacker was a two-time All-ACC machine. After college he was drafted by the Colts as the ninety-third pick and was part of Baltimore's 2009 conference championship team.

Coaches

John Heisman

"When in doubt, punt"

The name *Heisman* is synonymous with the best player in college football. John Heisman was born on October 23, 1869 in Cleveland, Ohio and was the first paid coach in college football. He was also innovative; he came up with the snap, and he divided the game into quarters. In addition to these accomplishments, he led the charge for legalizing the forward pass. At a time when it was all about running plays and dozens of players would die in a season, one could say that allowing the forward pass may have saved football.

He came to Georgia Tech in 1904 and coached there for sixteen years. Before coming to Tech, Heisman played football at Brown University and earned a law degree from the University of Pennsylvania. In 1892 he set out on a head football coaching "tour" with Buchtel College, Auburn University, Clemson, and finally settled for a while with Tech. In the sixteen seasons in Atlanta, he led the Golden Tornado to four undefeated seasons and one national championship in 1917. His overall record with Tech is 102-29-7, the highest winning percentage of any coach for the Yellow Jackets. After Tech, he coached at the University of Pennsylvania, Washington and Jefferson University, and ended his career at Rice University.

Some of his innovations included:

- Originally the ball was rolled back to the quarterback until Heisman developed the center snap.
- The outlawed "hidden ball" trick of stuffing the ball under your shirt and running
- The audible "hike"
- The double lateral- quick pass to the running back who tosses it back to the quarterback
- Strongly petitioned to legalize the forward pass

William Alexander

How does one follow John Heisman? William Alexander was a calm and collected man, full of reasonability. He wore he same expression whether a game was a win or a loss. This attitude made him popular among the players and fans. He started out as an engineering student in 1906 but later became assistant coach, then head coach, and finally the athletic director. Never coaching anywhere else, he was Tech down to the bone.

'Coach Aleck' was born in Mud River Kentucky in 1889. He earned a degree in civil engineering at Georgia Tech. He played football under Heisman but found his niche on the sideline as an assistant coach. When Heisman left Atlanta in 1920, Alexander took over with big shoes to fill. In his first nine seasons, he led Tech to first place in conference standings five times. As Tech hit the bottom during the 1930s, one wouldn't know it by looking at Alexander; he just pressed on.

Under his belt, he had accumulated a National Championship in 1928, two Southern Intercollegiate Athletic Association championships, three Southern Conference championships, and three SEC championships. In 1939, Tech was 6-0 in the SEC and won the Orange Bowl. Alexander was SEC Coach of the Year.

Bobby Dodd

"We should always keep uppermost in mind that football, with all its glamour, glitter, thrills and chills, plus everything that makes it great, has one thing more important than all of these combined—that is, the boy who plays it."

Robert Lee Dodd was born in Galax, Virginia on November 11, 1908. He led the Tennessee Volunteers to a 27-1-2 record as quarterback, but shocked Tennessee fans when he joined the coaching staff of William Alexander at Tech in 1931.

Although his first season was a losing one, he only repeated that type of performance once more in his twenty-two years as the head coach. His reign as head coach lasted from 1945 to 1966 and earned him a record of 165-64-8. In the early 1950s, he led the Ramblin' Wreck to thirty-one consecutive wins. Not only that, but to the disgust of Georgia fans, Tech held on to an eight game winning streak against UGA from 1946 to 1954.

After giving up the throne in 1966, he stayed on as the athletic director until 1976. He passed away in 1988, and Georgia Tech named the stadium surrounding Grant Field Bobby Dodd Stadium in his honor. He is a member of the College Football Hall of Fame as both a coach and a player.

Georgia Southern

Eagles Football began in 1924 and lasted until the onset of World War II. The school suspended its football program until 1981, but entered NCAA I-AA officially in 1984. They hired the UGA's former defensive coordinator, Erk Russell in 1982 and the Eagles soared to a Division I-AA national championship in 1985, beating Furman University. Russell retired in 1989 after another national championship. Tom Stowers led Georgia Southern to yet another championship and was named Coach of the Year. After five years, Stowers was fired, and the next year was the school's first losing season since it reinstated the football program. With help from Adrian Peterson, the Eagles made it to another national championship in 1998 but lost. Apparently the team didn't care for that loss, so the players decided to win in 1999 and 2000. Georgia Southern will move to the Sun Belt Conference in 2014 and hopefully win some bowl games.

Legends

Tracy Ham

Tracy Ham was a versatile quarterback at Georgia Southern and became a Canadian football star. He played for the Eskimos, Argonauts, Stallions, and Alouettes. For the Eskimos, he set records for most passing touchdowns in a season and most rushing yards for a quarterback. After retiring, he came back to Georgia to coach a Clark Atlanta University. Ham was inducted into the Canadian Football Hall of Fame in 2010.

"Captain" Bill Winn

Bill Winn was a special talent from Atlanta, Georgia, excelling in multiple sports, including football, track, tennis, and basketball. He could play any position in football and acted as Georgia Southern's kicker, running back, receiver, return specialist, and even safety.

Erskine "Erk" Russell

For seventeen years during some of the Georgia Bulldogs best years, Russell was the team's defensive coordinator. When Georgia Southern decided to bring back its football program, the school asked Russell if he'd help rebuild. Rebuild he did, because he brought the team a Division I-AA national championship three times in his eight years with the Eagles. His overall record with Georgia Southern was 83-22-1.

Mercer University

The Bears were an early member of the Southern Intercollegiate Athletic Association. The team played the first intercollegiate football game in Georgia, against UGA, but lost 50-0. They pulled it together and beat Tech in their next game. Mercer became part of the Dixie Conference, but dismantled its sports program during World War II. When athletics started back up in 1948, the school decided to leave out football. The Bears record holder for points scored was Joseph Smith, who is a member of the Georgia Sports Hall of Fame. Football was finally reinstated in 2013, when the Bears joined the Pioneer Football League.

Professional Football

A school teacher from Griffin, Georgia picked the nickname Falcons in 1965. She said, "the falcon is proud and dignified, with great courage and fight. It never drops its prey. It is deadly and has a great sporting tradition." Other choices for the new team were the Confederates, Firebirds, Peaches, and the Thrashers.

The Falcons' story goes back to Ivan Allen Jr. and the 'Forward Atlanta' initiative, which sought to bring more business to Hotlanta. Part of 'Forward Atlanta' involved building a stadium and attracting a professional sports team to move to the Gate City. An expansion team, Rankin Smith secured the Falcons for $8.5 million. There were attempts by the AFL to get a team in Atlanta, but the league had to settle for Miami instead.

The Falcons struggled for several seasons and didn't win until they beat the New York Giants in their tenth game. Their first two seasons had a combined record of 4-23-1 under Coach Norb Hecker. In their first five seasons, the Falcons' record was below .500, and then in 1971 the team made it over the hump with a 7-6-1 record. With Norm Van Brocklin, the team didn't improve much and compiled a 38-57-3 record in seven years.

It wasn't until 1978 that the Birds made it to the playoffs with help from Steve Bartkowski and some last minute heroics in the wildcard race. Under Coach Leeman Bennett, the Falcons had a six-season record of 46-41, with three second-place finishes and their first division title in 1980. After a strike-shortened season in 1982, Bennett was fired and eight losing seasons followed.

With new black uniforms and unique coach Jerry Glanville, the Falcons started the 1990s off with a bang, which sounds nice, but the truth was that it took a year for the Birds to regain that winning spirit of the early 1980s. In 1991, the Falcons beat the Saints for the wildcard position in the NFC divisional playoffs. Atlanta lost to the Redskins, thus, ending their "back in black" run. After two 6-10 seasons to follow, the Falcons fired Glanville and the Falcons hired June Jones to bring some dignity to Atlanta. This was not to be, but in 1997 the Falcons hired someone with Super Bowl experience and a history in Georgia.

Dan Reeves was born in Rome, Georgia, in 1944 and had quite a career with the Cowboys as a running back. He coached the Broncos to three Super Bowls, but unfortunately the Broncos just couldn't win. After four seasons with the Giants, Atlanta picked him up for the 1997 season. His first year was a rebuilding one and the Falcons lost the first five games but won five of the last six. In 1998 and after 32 seasons, Atlanta finally reached the ultimate game in football, the Super Bowl. With Reeves undergoing quadruple bypass surgery and coaching shortly afterward, it was a hard road to the top. Jamal Anderson's 1846 rushing yards and his "Dirty Bird" dance in the end zone would not be enough for the Falcons, who lost to the Broncos 19-34.

After three seasons under .500, Reeves was able to bring one more decent season to Atlanta in 2002. But they lost in playoffs, and Reeves lasted only part of the next year. The Falcons made adjustments in the years after Reeves and went through their share of coaches, including Wade Phillips, Jim Mora, Bobby Petrino, and Emmitt Thomas. In 2008, the Falcons seemed to have found their man, Mike Smith.

After going 11-5 in their first year with Smith, the Dirty Birds have had winning seasons up to this writing in 2013. Unfortunately, each time the Falcons reached the playoff potential, they lost in the wildcard game. In five seasons with Smith, the Falcons have come in second place three times and first place twice. The time for a Super Bowl win is so close, so close.

Falcon Facts

- It took ten years for the Falcons to have a 1,000-yard rusher: Dave Hampton.

- It took fifteen years for a Falcon quarterback to pass more than 3000 yards: Steve Bartkowski.

- Only two Falcons have thrown for more than 4,000 yards in a season: Jeff George and Matt Ryan.

- Morten Andersen holds the Falcon record for the longest field goal: 59 yards.

- Roddy White is the only Falcon to reach more than 200 passing yards in a game, which he did twice.

- Two Falcons have rushed for more than 200 yards in a game: Gerald Riggs and Michael Turner, who did it twice.

- Todd McClure holds the Falcons record for most consecutive games started: 144.
- In 1993, Bobby Hebert made the longest pass completion: 98 yards.
- In 1978, Wallace Francis became the first receiver to reach more than 1,000.
- The record for tackles in a season -296- was set by Tommy Nobis in 1966.
- Jerious Norwood's 2,207 all-purpose yards is a Falcons record: 613 yards rushing, 277 receiving, and 1,317 yards in kick-off returns.
- The Falcons best record was in 1998: 14-2
- The most points the Falcons scored in a game was 62 in 1973 against the Saints.
- Their overall record is 312-402 in 47 seasons as of the 2012 season.

Legends
William Andrews

William Andrews was born on Christmas day in 1955, in Thomasville, Georgia. What is so special about Andrews is that he did so much in such a short time. He played for the Falcons from 1979 to 1983, with a limited comeback in 1986. After playing for Auburn, he was selected by the Falcons as the seventy-ninth pick in the 1979 NFL draft. He was a Pro Bowl selection four years in a row, from 1980 to 1983. His best season was in 1983, when he rushed for 1567 yards and had more than 600 yards receiving.

Unfortunately, in the 1984 preseason, Andrews sustained a nasty knee injury that would put his career on hold for two years. Overcoming his "career-ending" injury, he played again in 1986 but retired after the season. He was inducted into the Falcon's Ring of Honor in 2004, and in 2006 he was inducted into the Georgia Sports Hall of Fame.

G	Ru Yd	TDs	Rec Yards	Rec TDs
87	5986	30	2647	11

Steve Bartkowski

Steve Bartkowski was born on November 12, 1952 in Des Moines, Iowa. In three years with the Golden Bears he threw for 4,434 yards, made 313 completions on 619 attempts, and threw 20 touchdowns. He was an All-American selection in 1974, when he threw for more than 2500 yards and had 12 touchdown passes. Bartkowski was no one-trick pony, as he was also an All-American baseball player for UC Berkeley. In 1975, he was the first selection in the NFL draft by the Falcons.

In his first year with Atlanta he was the NFL Rookie of the Year and threw thirteen touchdowns (we won't speak of the fifteen interceptions). By 1980 he was a full blown star, reaching more than 3,500 passing yards and 31 touchdowns in said year. He topped the yardage the next year with over 3800 and thirty touchdown passes. Not too shabby.

In eleven seasons with the Falcons (1975 to 1985) he set practically every franchise passing record. Matt Ryan is quickly chasing down those records, but Bartkowski still holds plenty. He was the 1978 NFL MVP, a Pro Bowl selection in 1980 and 1981, and was inducted into the Georgia Sports Hall of Fame.

G	Com%	Yds	TDs	INT
129	55.9	24124	156	144

Jim Brown (Georgia Native)

Most people know Jim Brown as the stalker Fireball from *The Running Man*, which also starred Arnold Schwarzenegger. Others may know him as Slammer from *I'm Gonna Git You Sucka*. Only a few people know that Jim Brown was one of the best professional football players of all time. *A few?*

Brown was born on February 17, 1936, on St. Simons Island, Georgia. After a First-Team All-American season in his senior year at Syracuse, he was drafted by the Cleveland Browns in 1956. He was a nine-time Pro Bowl selection, eight-time rushing champ, and three-time MVP. On top of all that, he averaged more than 104 yards a game, and broke practically all the rushing records that existed at the time.

Brown was inducted into the Pro Football Hall of Fame in 1971 and then surprisingly to the Lacrosse Hall of Fame. He once said, "I'd rather play lacrosse six days a week and football on the seventh." Fireball has been in more than forty films, participated in color commentary, and played pro football.

Pro Bowls: 1957-1965
Rushing Yards Leader : 1958, 1959, 1961, 1963, 1964, 1965

G	R Yards	TDs	Rec Yards	Rec TDs
118	12312	106	2499	20

Tommy Nobis

Tommy Nobis was born on September 20, 1943, in San Antonio, Texas. "Mr. Falcon" was the first draft-pick for the new expansion team in Atlanta. He got his start at the University of Texas and won the Knute Rockne Award for best lineman and the Maxwell Award for best college player, all while dealing with a bad knee. In those days, individual statistics were not officially kept, especially for defense, so there is just no telling how amazing he truly was by the record books.

When he was selected as the number one pick in the 1966 NFL draft, he said, "The thing for me to do now is to live up to all this fine treatment and to do the job I'm expected to do." That is exactly what he did in the eleven years he donned a Falcons jersey. He was the defensive Rookie of the Year in 1966 and made the Pro Bowl five times (1966, 1967, 1968, 1970, and 1972). He is a member of the College, Georgia Sports, and University of Texas Halls of Fame. Why isn't Nobis in the Pro Football Hall of Fame? Great question—

Gerald Riggs

"RIGGS!" *as Danny Glover would yell*— He was born in Tullos, Louisiana, in 1960. Riggs played high school football in Las Vegas and then played from 1978 to 1981 for Arizona State. He amassed 18 total touchdowns and 2086 rushing yards as a Sun Devil. After his days in the sun, he was chosen by the Falcons as the ninth overall pick in the 1982 NFL draft.

After ten years in the NFL, Riggs recorded more than 8,000 rushing yards with the Falcons and the Redskins. The three-time Pro Bowler settled Atlanta's nerves after William Andrews' terrible injury. He finished his career with the Redskins and earned himself a Super Bowl ring when they defeated the Bills. Football runs in the family; he has two sons that have played in college.

G	R Yards	TDs	Rec Yards
129	8188	69	1516

Matt Ryan (Active)

Matt Ryan was born in Exton, Pennsylvania, on May 17, 1985. He played football, basketball, and baseball at William Penn Charter School and decided to take football all the way. He started out as a backup quarterback for Boston College and in his sophomore year he became the starter for the Eagles. After the 2007 season, he was the ACC Player of the Year, First-Team All-American, and he received the Manning Award and the Johnny Unitas Golden Arm Award.

Watch out Bartkowski— Ryan's coming for your records. Ryan has taken over numerous single-season records, like passing yards (4,719), pass completions (422, 357, and 347), pass attempts (615), and touchdowns (32). He is second on the Falcon's leader board in several categories. But what makes him incredible is that he has only played five seasons. "Matty Ice" was a Pro Bowl selection in 2010 and 2012, not to mention the Offensive Rookie of the Year in 2008. A Super Bowl ring is in his future...

G	Comp %	Yds	TDs	Int
78	62.7	18957	127	60

Deion Sanders

"Neon" Deion Sanders played college football under the legendary Bobby Bowden and was a three-time All-American cornerback. His jersey was retired in 1995. He was also a quick-running baseball player who was a phenomenal base stealer. Drafted by the Atlanta Falcons for football in 1989, he was also picked up by the New York Yankees the same year.

In baseball, Sanders played for a number of teams including the Yankees, the Braves (1991-1994), the Reds, and the Giants. He stole 186 bases in his career and hit 43 triples. Because he was a two-sport star, he never played more than 97 (out of 162) games in a season, so his numbers are lower than they could have been.

It was his football career that made him legendary, with eight Pro-Bowl selections and eight All-Pro selections. He was a two-time NFC Defensive Player of the Year and holds the NFL record for the most defensive touchdowns with nineteen. Sanders is a member of the College and Pro Football Hall of Fame and is part of the Falcons Ring of Honor.

G	P R Yds	P R TDS	K Ret. Yds	Int	Int Tds	Tkl
188	2199	6	3523	53	9	492

Jessie Tuggle

Jessie "The Hammer" Tuggle was an unstoppable force on the Falcons' defense for fourteen seasons. He went to college at Valdosta State University in southern Georgia and starred on the line for the Blazers. He had the nickname "Rag Doll" because that's what the other players looked like when he hit them.

His career with the Falcons led him to the Super Bowl in 1998 and five Pro Bowls. He was a three-time All-Pro, and his number 58 was retired by the Falcons. Tuggle holds the Falcons franchise record for career tackles with 1,640; 694 more than the next closest linebacker in the record books. He has a son playing football in college as well as a daughter who attends his alma mater and plays tennis. "Rag Doll" was inducted into the College Football Hall of Fame in 2007 and became a member of the Falcons Ring of Honor in its inaugural class in 2004.

G	Sacks	Fmb Ret TDs	Tkls
209	21	5	1640

Jeff Van Note

The center from South Orange, New Jersey, played with the Falcons from 1969 to 1986. A forty-year-old center sounds unbelievable, doesn't it? Van Note lost his mother when he was eleven, and according to the December 8, 1983, *Harlan Daily Enterprise* he said, "I started playing football to fill a void…Now I keep playing it because I'm one of the luckiest people in the world to have a job where you get five months a year off."

The six-time Pro Bowler was selected in 1974, 1975, 1979, 1980, 1981, and 1982. His jersey number 57 was retired at his final home game in 1986, and he became part of the Falcon's Ring of Honor in 2006.

Roddy White (Active)

"Rowdy" Roddy White was born on James Island, South Carolina, on November 2, 1981. While in college, he tinkered with a few sports and managed to letter in football, soccer, wrestling, and baseball. Lettering in four sports hasn't been seen much since before the war. *Which war?* He was picked by the Falcons as the twenty-seventh choice in the 2005 NFL draft.

(Spoiler Alert: Record-breaker ahead) White has been with the Falcons since he was drafted in 2005. Since then he has broken the single-game record for receiving yardage with 210. He also holds the Falcons record for career receiving yardage with 7,374 and the most seasons with 1,000 or more yards (six, as of 2012). So far, he has been a Pro Bowl selection four times and was All-Pro in 2010. There are bound to be more records to break in the years ahead of him.

G	Rec	Yards	TDs
128	622	8725	52

Notable Falcons

John Abraham

After playing college ball for the University of South Carolina, he was drafted by the New York Jets in 2000 and stayed there for six years. He was traded to the Falcons in 2006 and became one of the best defensive ends the Falcons had ever seen. After just six years, Abraham holds the team record for career sacks with 68.5. He has a total of 122 sacks, 508 tackles, and 44 forced fumbles in his career.

Arthur Blank

Blank co-founded Home Depot in 1978, which resulted in him becoming a billionaire. With a bit more change in his pocket than normal he made a small purchase in 2002: the Atlanta Falcons. He has expressed interest in an expansion team ownership in Major League Soccer, but for now let's just hope his Falcons can win a Super Bowl.

Greg Brezina

This linebacker spent twelve seasons with the Falcons from 1968 to 1979. After battling with alcohol, he became a born-again Christian. Unfortunately, tackles and sacks were not something the league recorded, so no one will know his official tally. He was one of the greats—.

Keith Brooking

Georgia Tech warrior Keith Brooking made his way to the Falcons and was a standout linebacker for eleven years. For more information see the Georgia Tech football section.

Warren Bryant

Bryant was a tackle for the Atlanta Falcons from 1977 to 1984 and for the Los Angeles Raiders in 1984. He attended the University of Kentucky and was picked by the Falcons in the first round of the 1977 draft. He struggled with drugs and alcohol throughout his career

Bobby Butler

A cornerback from Florida State, Bobby Butler was picked by the Falcons twenty-fifth in the 1981 draft. He played for Atlanta from 1981 to 1992 and co-founded a non-profit youth football camp called Kids & Pros with another former Falcon, Buddy Curry.

Scott Case

After attending Oklahoma in the early 1980s, Scott Case was drafted by the Falcons in the second round. Case was a defensive back for the Falcons from 1984 to 1994 and a Pro Bowl selection in 1988, the year he led the league in interceptions, with ten.

Chris Chandler

Chris Chandler played with the Colts, Bucs, Cardinals, Rams, Oilers, Falcons, Bears, and Rams (this time in St. Louis). But his longest stint was in Atlanta. He helped lead the team to their first Super Bowl in 1998. His only Pro Bowl appearances were with the Falcons in 1997 and 1998.

Alge Crumpler

Algernon Darius Crumpler was the tight end for the Atlanta Falcons for seven years and later played with the Titans and Patriots. After playing in college for the University of North Carolina, the Falcons picked him thirty-fifth in the 2001 draft. He made the Pro Bowl four times from 2003 to 2006.

Buddy Curry

Buddy Curry, born in Greenville, North Carolina, was a star linebacker for the Atlanta Falcons for eight years starting in 1980. He was the Defensive Rookie of the Year and a two-time All-Pro selection. In 2002 he started a youth football camp called Kids & Pros, where the instructors are all NFL players.

Warrick Dunn

Dunn made his start with the Buccaneers but spent six glorious years with the Falcons. He reached more 10,000 rushing yards in his career, was a three-time Pro Bowl selection, and was Offensive Rookie of the Year in 1997. Known for his work off the field, he has been honored with the Walter Payton Man of the Year Award and the Bart Starr Man of the Year Award for his good character and charity work.

Bill Fralic

Bill Fralic played eight years with the Birds as an offensive guard. He was the second overall pick in the 1985 NFL draft. As his career progressed, he was a two-time All-Pro in 1986 and 1987, and a Pro Bowl selection four years in a row starting in 1986. Never one to juice up, he spoke out against all the steroid use that was happening in the NFL in a United States Senate hearing in 1989.

Travis Hall

Hall was a Falcon for ten years and played one more year with the 49ers. The defensive tackle from Soldotna, Alaska played ball at Brigham Young University in Utah. He reached more than 450 tackles in his career, with forty-two sacks, and is fourth on the Falcons' sacks record list.

Don Hansen

Don Hansen played for twelve years in the NFL with such teams as the Vikings, the Falcons, the Seahawks, and the Packers. His longest stint was the seven years he spent with the Falcons. The fierce linebacker delivered devastating hits and many consider him to be quite underrated. After playing for the Vikings, he quit football to sell real estate. When he didn't sell anything, he signed with the Falcons and was voted the team's MVP by his teammates.

Claude Humphrey

Born in Memphis in 1944, Claude Humphrey was the third pick in the 1968 NFL draft. After his first season in Atlanta, he was the Defensive Rookie of the Year. He played defensive end for eleven seasons with the Falcons. Not surprisingly, he was a Pro Bowl selection six times and a five-time, First-Team All-Pro selection. Humphrey is a member of the Georgia and Tennessee sports hall of fame.

Alfred Jenkins

Alfred Jenkins was a wide receiver for the Falcons from 1975 to 1983. The two-time Pro Bowler accumulated forty touchdowns and 360 receptions in his career. He held the franchise season reception record (1358) until broken by Roddy White. With 6267 reception yards, he is third on the Falcons' career leaders list.

Billy 'White Shoes' Johnson

Billy Johnson was known for his gleaming white shoes and was one of the first players to dance in the end zone. He played for the Oilers for seven years and a year in Canada before joining the Falcons in 1982. In his six years with Atlanta, he was a Pro Bowl selection and the NFL Comeback Player of the Year in 1983. Used mainly as a kick returner, he also played wide receiver in Atlanta and twice led the team in receptions.

Mike Kenn

Born on February 9th, 1956, Mike Kenn was a tackle for the Falcons from 1978 to 1994. Kenn has yet to be surpassed in the category of games started, for the Falcons, with 251. He was a Pro Bowl selection in 1980, 1981, 1982, and 1984, and was First-Team All-Pro in 1980, 1983, and 1991. His number, 78, is retired in Atlanta.

Patrick Kerney

Patrick Kerney was a defensive end for the Falcons from 1999 to 2006. He attended the University of Virginia and was selected in the first round of the 1999 NFL draft. Kerney was a Pro Bowl selection twice and was the NFC Defensive Player of the Year (after he left the Falcons—). In his career, he has 401 tackles and 82.5 sacks in eleven years of NFL play.

George Kunz

George Kunz was 1968 First-Team All-American while a tackle for Notre Dame. He was the second overall pick by the Falcons in the 1969 NFL draft. An eight-time Pro-Bowl selection, Kunz was one of the top Falcon's defenders of the 1970s.

Fulton Kuykendall

Fulton Kuykendall was a linebacker for UCLA before the Falcons took him in the 1975 draft as their 132nd pick. He played with the Falcons from 1975 to 1984. He was known to put himself in career-ending situations on the field on a regular basis, and for this his teammates nicknamed him "Kaptain Krazy".

Rolland Lawrence

Rolland Lawrence was a cornerback for the Falcons from 1973 to 1980. He holds the franchise record for interceptions (39) and interception yards (658). He was a three-time Pro Bowl selection and in 1975 returned an eighty-seven-yard interception for a touchdown.

Terance Mathis

Terance Mathis was one of the best wide receivers in the Falcons' history. He got his start in Atlanta in 1994 and played with the team until 2001. Mathis is second in total reception yards in franchise history, behind Roddy White, with 7,349 yards. He is currently the Falcon's all-time reception touchdown leader with fifty-seven.

Todd McClure

The former LSU center was the 237th pick in the 1999 NFL draft. Todd McClure was born in Baton Rouge, Louisiana on February 16, 1977. He has been the Falcon's starting center since the year 2000.

Chris Miller

Chris Miller was born on August 9, 1965 in Pomona, California. He was the quarterback for the Oregon Ducks and was the thirteenth pick in the 1987 NFL draft. Miller played with the Falcons until 1993. He is third in career-passing yards for the Falcons with 14,066, and third in touchdowns with eighty-seven.

Jim R. Mitchell

Jim Mitchell played from 1969 to 1979 with the Falcons and didn't play for another team in his career. He was a two-time Pro Bowl selection at tight end. After his career, he went on to coach at Morehouse College and Morris Brown College in Atlanta.

Ken Reaves

Ken Reaves was born in Braddock, Pennsylvania on October 29th, 1944. After attending Norfolk State he was picked in the fourth round, the forty-ninth overall selection, of the 1966 NFL draft. He was a defensive back in Atlanta from the team's inception to 1973.

Andre Rison

Andre Rison packed a big punch in a short amount of time as the Falcons wide receiver from 2000 to 2004. He still retains the record for receptions average per game, at 5.4. He is third for receptions on the Falcon's leader board with 423 and fourth in yardage with 5,633. These stats are even more remarkable given that he played at least forty-two games less than those above him. Many remember when Lisa Lopes burned his shoes in the tub and the fire destroyed everything that he owned. They stayed together. Ahh, love.

Allen Rossum

Rossum is another one of those players who isn't talked about too much, but was an incredible threat on the field. He played on several teams in his career, but his four years with the Falcons were some of his best. In that short amount of time he set franchise records for career kickoff-return yardage (1,723), punt return yardage (5,489), all-purpose yardage (7,212), kickoff returns (250), and punt returns (154).

Chuck Smith

Chuck Smith was born in Athens, Georgia, and played defensive end at the University of Tennessee. After college he was the fifty-first pick of the 1992 NFL draft by the Atlanta Falcons. Smith played in Atlanta until 1999 and was an All-Pro selection in 1997. He recorded 58.5 sacks in his career and later went on to coach for the Volunteers in Tennessee.

R. C. Thielemann

R. C. Thielemann was born in Houston, Texas, on August 12th, 1955. He attended the University of Arkansas (playing guard) and was picked up by the Falcons in the 1977 NFL draft in the second round. R. C. played in Atlanta from 1977 to 1984 and was a Pro Bowl selection in 1981, 1982, and 1983.

Michael Turner

After several years as the back-up for LaDainian Tomlinson on the Chargers, Michael Turner signed with the Falcons in 2008, and no one ever looked back. *Isn't that what we just did?* Turner holds the Falcon's single-game rushing record with 220 yards. He also holds the franchise record for career rushing touchdowns with sixty and rushing touchdowns in a season with seventeen. After a season of injuries in 2012, Turner was released by the Falcons to make room for Jacquizz Rodgers, perhaps.

Michael Vick

I'll leave out the thing that everyone is thinking about. *[cough] dogfights [cough]* He probably would've fit right in during Georgia's bearbaiting and bullbaiting colonial years. All of that aside, Michael Vick was one of the best quarterbacks in the history of the Falcons. It wasn't that he was the best passer, but it was his versatility and ability to run the ball that made him so special. There. His football ability has been mentioned.

Jeff Yeates

Jeff Yeates was born on August 3, 1951, in Buffalo, New York. He played defensive end for Boston College and was the 103rd pick of the 1973 NFL draft by the Buffalo Bills. Later, he played with the Falcons from 1976 to 1984.

Notable Georgians

George Atkinson

Born in Savannah in 1947, George Atkinson attended Morris Brown College in Atlanta. His career spanned from 1968 to 1977 and he played for the Oakland Raiders and the Denver Broncos. He's a three-time Pro Bowl selection and was part of Oakland's winning Super Bowl XI team. Moreover, he had thirty career interceptions and set the NFL record for punt return yards in a game with 205.

Mel Blount

Born in Toombs County, Georgia in 1948, Mel Blount attended college at Southern University in Louisiana. He played in the NFL for fourteen years, solely for the Pittsburgh Steelers. Blount was a Pro Bowl selection in 1975, 1976, 1978, 1979, and 1981. He was named to the 1980s All-Decade Team and holds four Super Bowl rings. The Pro Football Hall of Fame inducted Blount in 1989, and he's been inducted into the Louisiana and Georgia Sports Hall of Fame as well.

Emerson Boozer

Emerson Boozer was born in Augusta, Georgia in 1942 and attended college at Maryland Eastern Shore. He played for the Jets from 1966 to 1975 as a running back, was All-Pro in 1967, and a Pro-Bowl selection in 1966 and 1968. He scored 52 touchdowns and compiled 5,135 yards over his career. The Georgia Sports Hall of Fame inducted Boozer in 1991.

Bobby Lee Bryant

Macon, Georgia-native Bobby Lee Bryant was born in 1944 and attended the University of South Carolina. Picked in the late rounds of the 1967 NFL draft by the Minnesota Vikings, the defensive back had a quality thirteen-year career. His fifty-one career interceptions and fourteen fumble recoveries helped the Vikings win four Super Bowls and eleven division championships. On another note, he could have played baseball in the pros, but chose football instead.

Earnest Byner

Earnest Byner, a running back from Milledgeville, Georgia, was born in 1962 and played fourteen years in the NFL. He coached for teams including the Ravens, Redskins, Titans, Jaguars, and Buccaneers. He compiled 56 touchdowns and 8261 rushing yards in his career. Because of his receptions, Byner reached 13,442 all-purpose yards, and managed 33 kickoff returns.

Richard Dent

Atlanta native Richard Dent attended Tennessee State, and was picked in the eighth round in the 1983 NFL draft. Dent was a defensive end for the Bears for eleven years, and also played for the 49ers, Colts, and Eagles. He is currently seventh on the all-time sacks list in the NFL. In 2009, Dent was inducted into the Pro Football Hall of Fame, having been inducted into the Georgia Sports Hall of Fame the previous year.

William Ray Guy

Although not a Falcon, Guy was from Swainsboro, Georgia, and played football for the Raiders from 1973 to 1986. He was a Pro Bowl selection seven times, and a Super Bowl champ three times. Oh yeah, he was a punter. He's a member of the Georgia Sports Hall of Fame.

Tommy Hart

Tommy Hart, from Macon, Georgia, attended Morris Brown College in Atlanta. The defensive end played in the NFL from 1968 to 1980 with the 49ers, Bears, and Saints. "Tommy Boy" was All-Pro in 1976 with the 49ers and has more than 130 unofficial sacks in his career (sacks were not recorded by the NFL until 1982). After his playing career, Hart coached for the Cowboys and the 49ers as a defensive end coach.

Cam Newton

What, Cam Newton? That's right, Cam Newton. He was born in Atlanta, Georgia, and attended Westlake High School. He was the Heisman Trophy winner in 2010 and has since torn up the field with the Carolina Panthers. Newton was the Offensive Rookie of the Year and set an NFL record with fourteen rushing touchdowns as a quarterback.

Jim Parker

Jim Parker was born in Macon, Georgia on April 3, 1934. Recognized as one of the best offensive linemen of all time, Parker is in both the Pro Football and College halls of fame. He played football during his first three high school years in Macon, but moved to Ohio for his senior year. The All-American attended Ohio State and was picked by the Baltimore Colts in the 1957 NFL draft. He was a Pro-Bowl selection eight times and All-Pro ten times.

Billy Paschal

Billy Paschal was born in Atlanta on May 28, 1921. A knee injury cut short his time at Georgia Tech, so he went to the work for the railroad. After some time, he was able to try out for professional football and was signed by the New York Giants in 1943. He led the league in rushing twice during the 1940s and was an All-Pro once. You didn't want to be hit by Paschal on or off the field. He was once charged with assault with a deadly weapon, but the charges were reduced when the "deadly weapon" turned out to be his fist.

George Rogers

George Washington Rogers was born in Duluth, Georgia, on December 8, 1958. After becoming an All-American running back at the University of South Carolina, he won the Heisman Trophy in 1980. He was the first pick in the 1981 NFL draft by the Saints. Rogers only played for seven seasons, but they were remarkable years in the pros. He brought the Saints out of the gutter, and later earned a Super Bowl ring with the Redskins. In just seven seasons he ran for 7,176 yards and scored fifty-four touchdowns. He is a member of the Georgia and College Football Halls of Fame.

Clarence Scott

Clarence Scott was born in Atlanta on April 9, 1949. His speed and agility allowed him to be a successful safety for the Browns for thirteen years during the 1970s and 1980s. After a great career at Kansas State, he was picked up by the Browns in the 1971 NFL draft. He totaled thirty-nine interceptions and was an All-Pro selection in 1973.

Shannon Sharpe

Growing up in Glenville, Georgia, Shannon Sharpe attended Savannah State College in the late 1980s. He was an All-Southern Intercollegiate Athletic Conference selection three times and also excelled at basketball and track and field. Good thing he chose the football route; he was a Pro Bowl selection eight times and was First-Team All-Pro four times. He set many records at the tight-end position, like being the first one to reach 10,000 receiving yards. Sharpe was a Super Bowl champion three times and was inducted into the Pro Football Hall of Fame in 2011.

James 'J. T.' Thomas

The defensive back was born in Macon, Georgia, on April 22nd, 1951. He dominated the field for Florida State University in the early 1970s, and was drafted by the Steelers in 1973 as the 24th overall pick. Thomas played in the NFL for ten seasons, and was a Pro Bowl selection in 1976.

Rayfield Wright

Wright was born in Griffin, Georgia, in 1945. He was an offensive tackle for the Dallas Cowboys from 1967 to 1980. "The Big Cat" was a six-time Pro Bowl selection and was All-Pro four times. He is a member of the Pro, Georgia Sports, and Texas Sports Halls of Fame.

<u>6</u>

— Basketball —

Way Back When

Peach Basket

The original goal was a basket...*duh*. Whether it was a basket or a net, there was no opening for about the first fifteen years of the game. Someone would get it out after every basket.

Soccer Time

The first few years of basketball's existence included the use of a soccer ball.

SILENCE!

Coaches weren't allowed to talk to players during a timeout for the first fifty years.

Bank Shot?

For the first five years, there was no backboard. Fans would also interfere with the shot and afterward hit it in a particular direction.

Nine versus Nine

The game originally had nine people on each side. James Naismith designed it this way, because he had eighteen students in his PE class.

Dribble

Dribbling was illegal in the beginning. When someone passed the ball, the player stopped. Eventually dribbling once was allowed, but if after dribbling, the player couldn't shoot.

Block the Goal!

Goaltending was legal until 1944.

Jump Ball again!

For the first forty-five years, there was a jump ball after every shot scored.

You Camping Out?

The three-second rule wasn't introduced until 1944.

Three Points?

"The score is 98 to 95. A shot from thirty feet out with one second on the buzzer... It's in!!! A two-pointer for the loss..." The three-point field goal wasn't introduced to the NBA until 1979.

I'll Shoot that Free Throw ...Again

It was common for one player (obviously the best shooter) to shoot all the free throws for the team.

Out of Bounds?

The first games were played with fencing or a "cage" around the court, preventing the ball from going out of bounds.

The Score: 26 to 19

Scores were very low for the first thirty years due to the absence of a shot clock. Players passed the ball over and over. Quite the slow pace.

Tons of Spud Webbs

The game didn't start out as a tall person's game. The average player's height for around the first thirty years was less than six feet tall.

History

At one point in James Naismith's career in physical education he needed to come up with a non-contact sport that could be played indoors during the brutal winter. How about tossing a ball into basket? Okay, that'll work.

There's a bit more to it, but that sums it up about a fast as anyone could. Basketball is different from other team sports in that it can be traced to a single person, Naismith, who invented the game in 1891.

Naismith figured that he had to come up with something new and decided on a non-contact sport that would require finesse. One could thank a game called ducks on a rock, which required good aim and the ability to avoid being tagged. The object of this adolescent game was to throw rocks at the guard's stone (the duck) which was placed on a boulder of some sort. If you went to retrieve your rock, the guard would try to tag you. Naismith recalled that the best method to knock the stone off was to throw with an arc. This led him to develop a horizontal goal instead a vertical ground-level one.

The school's janitor provided him with a couple of peach baskets and the game was almost set.

Next, Naismith needed the rules for the game, and this is what he came up with:

1. The ball may be thrown in any direction with one or both hands.
2. The ball may be batted in any direction with one or both hands, but never with the fist.
3. A player cannot run with the ball. The player must throw it from the spot on which he catches it, allowance to be made for a man running at good speed.
4. The ball must be held by the hands. The arms or body must not be used for holding it.
5. No shouldering, holding, pushing, striking, or tripping in any way of an opponent. The first infringement of this rule by any person shall count as a foul; the second shall disqualify him until the next goal is made or, if there was evident intent to injure the person, for the whole of the game. No substitution shall be allowed.
6. A foul is striking at the ball with the fist, violations of Rules 3 and 4, and such as described in Rule 5.
7. If either side makes three consecutive fouls it shall count as a goal for the opponents (consecutive means without the opponents in the meantime making a foul).
8. A goal shall be made when the ball is thrown or batted from the grounds into the basket and stays there, providing those defending the goal do no touch or disturb the goal. If the ball rests on the edges, and the opponent moves the basket, it shall count as a goal.
9. When the ball goes out of bounds, it shall be thrown into the field and played by the first person touching it. In case of dispute, the umpire shall throw it straight into the field. The thrower-in is allowed five seconds. If he holds it longer, it shall go to the opponent. If any side persists in delaying the game, the umpire shall call a foul on them.
10. The umpire shall be the judge of the men and shall note the fouls and notify the referee when three consecutive fouls have been made. He shall have power to disqualify men according to Rule 5.
11. The referee shall be judge of the ball and shall decide when the ball is in play, in bounds, to which side it belongs, and shall keep the time. He shall decide when a goal has been made and keep account

of the goals, with any other duties that are usually performed by a referee.

12. The time shall be two fifteen-minute halves, with five minutes rest between.

13. The side making the most goals in that time shall be declared the winner.

The closest Georgia came to national attention in the first half of professional basketball was having its name in the song, "Sweet Georgia Brown," the Harlem Globetrotters' theme song. Part of this has to do with the fact that basketball's origin was in the North and it took some time for this regional game to spread over the country.

It was just a little slow to catch on in the South. Looking at the sports section of a local Atlanta newspaper in the late 1800s and early 1900s, basketball was hardly mentioned. There were organized teams through the YMCA, and eventually colleges and universities formed clubs. But it took time for a following to transpire.

According to the *Atlanta Georgian* on November 28, 1906: "The Y.M.C.A. has...called a meeting for Friday night...to make plans for the organization of a city basketball league. Among the teams which will probably be members...are Y.M.C.A, Atlanta Athletic Club, [Georgia] Tech, Atlanta Dental College, and the University School of Stone Mountain." *I'm betting on the dentists!*

In 1906, basketball generated a kick-start of enthusiasm in Georgia. But it was still considered a 'minor' sport like bowling and billiards. Baseball, football, golf, and boxing were the sports of the early twentieth century that dominated the news.

Just as the game was picking up, Georgia Tech did not produce a team for the 1911 season. As in most universities, most of the players were part of other sports clubs within their respective university. So, injuries sustained during the football season weren't going to help Tech win any basketball games. It could also be said that gymnasiums were not built, like they are today, with basketball in mind. Georgia Tech's gym had load bearing posts in the middle of what would be considered the court. *Talk about some serious yet hilarious injuries...*

University of Georgia

UGA's basketball team began in 1905 as a member of the Southern Intercollegiate Athletic Association. After a close game with Tech in 1906, the *Red and Black* reported that "plucky playing and good goal throwing characterize the work of our team." *Just like in today's papers...*

In 1921, UGA formed the Southern Conference with teams that included Clemson, Auburn, Alabama, Georgia Tech, Kentucky, NC State, UNC, Tennessee and Virginia.

The basketball team played home games in three-thousand-seat capacity Woodruff Hall from 1923 to 1964. In 1964, Stegeman Coliseum the "Stegesaurus" opened up. It seated more than ten-thousand people and is named for Herman Stegeman, UGA's former football and basketball coach. Under Stegeman, the basketball team set a still-unbroken record of thirteen wins in a row in 1931.

For the most part, UGA basketball has been average and overshadowed by the football program. The team's historical record is a tad above .500, but it has produced some excellent players and coaches. In its early years, from 1905 to 1919, the team had six coaches, including Walter Forbes, C. O. Heidler, W. A. Cunningham, Howell Peacock, Alfred Scott, and Kennon Mott. These first fifteen years were some of the best and the Bulldogs boasted a record of 69-25.

When Stegeman took over the team in 1919, he coached for twelve seasons with a record of 170-78. The next twenty years saw five coaches, all with records above .500. In 1952, Red Lawson took the reins and coached for next fourteen years. Why Lawson wasn't fired is beyond comprehension considering his overall record was 112-241.

The Bulldogs didn't improve with Ken Rosemond or John Guthrie. Combined, they coached for thirteen years and posted a 138-197 record. A breath of fresh air entered Athens in the form of Hugh Durham in 1979. In 1972, Durham led the Florida State Seminoles to the Final Four in the NCAA tournament. He was just what the Bulldogs needed and helped the Dawgs make the NCAA tournament five times in nine years, reaching the Final Four in 1983. The Bulldogs won the SEC tournament championship in that year and the SEC championship in 1990. The 1980s also produced two of

Georgia's greatest stars, Dominique Wilkins and Vern Fleming. In 1995, Durham retired with a 298-216 record.

The 1995-1996 season ushered in a new era, with the addition of coach Tubby Smith. His record in two years was 45-19, and the Bulldogs made it to the Sweet Sixteen in 1996. After the 1997 season, Smith was swept away by the University of Kentucky, where he was once an assistant coach. The Dawgs went through coaches Ron Jirsa and Jim Harrick before settling on Dennis Felton for six seasons. In 2008, UGA surprised the basketball world by winning the SEC tournament and making it to the NCAA tournament for the tenth time in Dawg history.

Felton was fired in 2009 after a long losing streak, and it seemed that UGA was going to have to start from scratch again. But Mark Fox took over coaching in 2009 and helped lead the team to the NCAA tournament in 2011. We'll just have to wait and see what the future holds for the Georgia basketball program.

Notables

Shandon Anderson

Shandon Anderson was born in Atlanta on New Year's Eve 1973. The 6'6" guard and forward played for the Bulldogs from 1992 to 1996. He had a successful career in the NBA playing for the Jazz, Rockets, Knicks, and the Heat. At Georgia, he averaged 12.8 points, 1.8 steals, 5 .0 rebounds, and 2.7 assists per game.

Willie Anderson

Willie Anderson played for the Bulldogs from 1984 to 1988 and was the tenth pick of the 1988 NBA draft. While at Georgia, he averaged 12.6 points per game, 1.3 steals, 1.1 blocks, 4.1 assists, and 3.9 rebounds. He played in the 1988 Olympics and received a bronze medal for America's third place finish. On top of it all, he played for eleven seasons in the NBA, averaging over 12 points per game.

Jacky Dorsey

Jacky Dorsey was born in 1954 and began his two years at UGA in 1974. Dorsey holds the Georgia record for scoring average in a career with 23.7 points per game and in a season with 25.7 points per game. Another record he holds is for field-goal attempts in game with 31. He was drafted by the New Orleans Jazz but only lasted a few seasons in the NBA.

Vern Fleming

Vern Fleming was an All-American point guard in 1983 and 1984 and received a gold medal in the 1984 Olympics in Los Angeles. While at Georgia he averaged 14.2 points per game, 1.6 steals, 3.2 assists, and 3.8 rebounds. He was picked up by the Pacers in the 1984 NBA draft as the eighteenth choice.

Sundiata Gaines

Sundiata Gaines was born in New York, on April 18, 1986. He averaged more than two steals per game and now holds the UGA record for career steals with 259. He is second on the Bulldog's all-time list for assists, with 476 from 2004 to 2008. Gaines went undrafted, but ended up playing for the Jazz, Timberwolves, Raptors, Nets. He now plays in the Chinese Basketball Association.

Litterial Green

Who holds the UGA record for points? Not Dominique, but Litterial Green, with 2,111. He was All-SEC in 1990, 1991, and 1992, and led the Dawgs to the SEC championship in 1990. After college he played for the Magic, Pistons, Bucks, and Cavaliers. In the twenty-first century he traveled the world, playing in Argentina, Puerto Rico, Turkey, Poland, and Slovenia.

Pat Hamilton

Pat Hamilton holds the UGA record for most steals in a season with eighty-nine, and he is second on the all-time Bulldog leader board for steals with 216. After college, he played for the Dallas Mavericks and the Cleveland Cavaliers, and he now directs youth basketball camps.

Jarvis Hayes

Jarvis Hayes is the twin brother of Jonas Hayes, the assistant coach for Georgia. He averaged more than eighteen points for the Bulldogs from 2001 to 2003, and was First-Team All-SEC twice. Hayes was drafted by the Washington Wizards as the tenth pick in 2003. He played there for five seasons and then for the Pistons and the Nets.

Jumaine Jones

Jumaine Jones, the "Thrilla from Camilla" was born in 1979 …not in Camilla, but in Florida. He averaged 16.6 points per game and nine rebounds as a Bulldog. The Hawks nabbed him with the twenty-seventh pick, but he was then traded to the 76ers and played for a variety of teams in the NBA until 2007. Since then, he's played professionally in Italy, Russia, Puerto Rico, and Israel.

Alec Kessler

Alex Kessler was an All-American in 1990. With 549 career free throws, he is the Bulldogs' all-time leader. He played for UGA from 1986 to 1990 and was the twelfth pick in the 1990 NBA draft by the Miami Heat. He did something not many players do after a basketball career; he became an orthopedic surgeon. Dr. Kessler passed away from a heart attack in 2007.

Bob Lienhard

Bob Lienhard was an All-American in 1969 and 1970. He set a Bulldog records for career rebounds with 1,116 and rebounds in a season with 396. In 1968, Lienhard set a school record against Sewanee by pulling down 32 rebounds in a single game. His career rebounding average was 14.9 from 1968 to 1970.

Zippy Morocco

Zippy Morocco was an All-American in 1953. He is tied with Morris Dinwiddie, Billy Rado, and Litterial Green for free throws made in a game with 16. He is the sole record holder for free throws made in a season with 210. Zippy averaged 23.6 points in 1953 and broke the SEC record for points in a season. Aside from basketball, he excelled at football, leading the Dawgs in kickoff returns for three years.

Dominique Wilkins

Dominique Wilkins is the biggest name to come out of the UGA basketball program. He averaged more than 21 points per game in about two and a half years as a Bulldog. 'Nique averaged 1.3 steals, 7.5 rebounds, and 1.8 blocks per game, and he holds the school record for points in a season (732) and field goals made in a career (723).

Georgia Tech

Georgia Tech's first official intercollegiate game was held on February 17, 1906 against Auburn University, with Tech losing 26-6. *Wow, quite the high scoring game...* Tech played Georgia twice, winning both times, but the second game was a tight race that Tech won 12-11 in sudden-death overtime. John Heisman was the coach for the basketball team starting in 1909, then William Alexander began coaching in 1919. At this time, basketball was more of a way to keep the football and baseball players in shape during the off-season.

The first truly permanent gym for the Tech boys to play in wasn't ready until the opening of the Heisman Gymnasium in 1938. Until then, they were playing in temporary gyms, the YMCA, the City Auditorium, St. Nicholas Rink, and the Naval Armory. Because of the lack of a gym, Tech was forced to shut down its basketball programs on several occasions until the 1919 season.

The 1930s may have been the era of the Great Depression, but you wouldn't know it by the way Tech played during this decade. At one point the team had a nineteen game winning streak, and were undefeated in the 1937 and 1938 seasons. Tech won the SEC title in 1938. Going through coaches Dwight Keith and Roy McArthur during the 1940s, 1951 marked the beginning of twenty-two years with coach John "Whack" Hyder.

During the 1950s Hyder developed Tech's basketball program into a well-oiled machine. One of the decade's most memorable moments of the decade came on January 8th, 1955. Up to this point, the Kentucky Wildcats were enjoying a home-court winning streak of 129 games. For twelve years they had not lost at home. Tech was 2-4 going into the game, and the Wildcats were looking ahead to their match-up against DePaul (real competition). Hyder only used his starting five players. Joe Helms, a 5'9" point guard, scored a jump shot to put Tech in the lead with 59 points to Kentucky's 58. When the game was over, the Tech players whooped and hollered, while the Kentucky fans were dead silent with looks of utter disbelief.

The 1960s started off with a bang as Roger Kaiser dominated the court and led Tech to its first NCAA tournament in 1960. In 1965, Georgia Tech left the SEC, but not before becoming the conference runner-up in the season prior. The 1970s brought several changes to the Yellow Jackets. Hyder retired after the 1972 season and was replaced by his assistant coach, Dwane Morrison, who coached until 1981. Tech moved into the Metro Conference in 1975 and to the Atlantic Coast Conference in 1978. Unfortunately for Morrison, Tech struggled badly in the ACC and compiled a 4-23 record in 1981.

Bobby Cremins took over for Morrison in 1981, the start of some of the best years in Tech history. Tech was soon back in form and won the 1985 conference tournament. Led by Mark Price and John Salley, the 1985 team also made it to the Elite Eight in the NCAA tournament. Tech participated in the NCAA tournament for nine consecutive seasons. They advanced to the Final Four in 1990, with help from the "Lethal Weapon Three" that included Kenny Anderson, Dennis Scott, and Danny Glover...I mean Brian Oliver.

After twenty years as head coach, Cremins retired in 2000 with a 354-237 record. Paul Hewitt took over and helped lead the team to the NCAA tournament finals, which, unfortunately, Tech would lose. Under Hewitt, Tech won a lot of games but struggled within their conference, where they tallied a 72-104 record from 2001 to 2011. Hewitt was fired and replaced by Tech's current coach, Brian Gregory.

Notables

Kenny Anderson

Born in Queens, New York in 1970, Kenny Anderson set the court on fire for Tech in 1990 and 1991. He helped lead the team to the Final Four in 1990, but Tech lost to UNLV. He was First-Team All-American in 1991. After playing only two seasons, he entered the NBA draft and was selected as the second overall pick by the New Jersey Nets. He played for fifteen years in the NBA with teams that included the Hornets, Trail Blazers, Celtics, SuperSonics, Pacers, Hawks, and the Clippers. Anderson is a member of the New York City Basketball Hall of Fame.

Jon Barry

Jon Barry is the son of the Rick Barry, who is in the NBA Hall of Fame. Born in California in 1969, Jon transferred to Georgia Tech in 1990 and played for two years for the Yellow Jackets. He averaged close to sixteen points a game in 1991 and seventeen points a game in 1992. Barry was selected in the first round of the NBA draft by the

Boston Celtics. He played fourteen years in the NBA with the Bucks, Warriors, Hawks, Lakers, Kings, Pistons, Nuggets and Rockets.

Travis Best

Point guard Travis Best played four years for Tech averaging 16.6 points and 5.6 assists per game. He led Tech to the 1993 ACC tournament win over the Tar Heels. Best was selected in the first round of the NBA draft by the Indiana Pacers and played for several years before moving to play in Europe.

George P. Burdell

What can be said about George P. Burdell? He holds numerous degrees, fought on many fronts in World War II, and was on the board of directors for *Mad Magazine*. Legend has it that he scored fifty points in a Tech game, but was not officially on the team. He's getting close to 100 years old, and Tech may sign him as the new assistant basketball coach. He's also a made-up person who has "been around" for dozens of years at Georgia Tech.

Al Ciraldo

Al Ciraldo was the sportscaster for the Ramblin' Wreck for 38 years. He was known for play-by-play that made a listener feel like he or she was live at the game. He not only announced football but held broadcast duties for basketball in the glory days of the 1980s and 1990s.

Bobby Cremins

Bobby Cremins coached the Yellow Jackets for twenty years and turned them from piss poor to a tournament team. He was the ACC Coach of the Year three times in 1983, 1985, and 1996, and he was the Naismith College Coach of the Year in 1990. His overall coaching record is 570-367, which includes taking over the coaching job for three subpar teams.

Tom Hammonds

Tom Hammonds was born in 1967, in Fort Walton, Florida. The 6'9" forward played for the Yellow Jackets from 1985 to 1989, averaging close to seventeen points and seven rebounds per game. He was the ninth overall selection in the 1989 NBA draft and played professionally for twelve years. Besides basketball, he delved into drag racing in the NHRA Pro Stock Division.

Matt Harpring

After attending Marist in Atlanta for high school, Matt Harpring began his college career with the Yellow Jackets in 1994 and was a First-Team All-ACC selection from 1996 to 1998. He averaged close to eighteen points and eight rebounds per game and was an All-American in his senior year. In 1998 he was the fifteenth overall pick in the NBA draft and played pro for twelve years, averaging 11.5 points per game.

William Waller "Tiny" Hearn

Tiny Hearn played for the Yellow Jackets at around the same time as Burdell (late 1920s), except Hearn was the real thing. He not only excelled at basketball but played some minor league baseball too. In 1992, he was inducted into the Georgia Sports Hall of Fame. "Tiny" was actually a giant at 6'9" and also played for the Tech football team as a tackle. He played during a time when basketball players were called basketeers. *I don't think today's players would go for that...*

Roger Kaiser

Born in 1939, Roger Kaiser was the point guard for Tech, and a First-Team All-American selection in 1960 and 1961. He led the SEC in scoring, and led Tech to its first NCAA tournament. After his playing career, he coached for close to twenty years at the University of West Georgia (formerly West Georgia College) and is a member of school's hall of fame.

Malcolm Mackey

Malcolm Mackey was born in 1970 in Chattanooga, Tennessee. He played for Tech from 1990 to 1993 and averaged thirteen points and nine rebounds per game. After his years with the Yellow Jackets, he was the twenty-seventh overall pick in the 1993 NBA draft by the Phoenix Suns but only played one season in the NBA. After this, he played all over the world for teams in Spain, Turkey, France, Puerto Rico, Greece, Italy, China, and Poland.

Stephon Marbury

Stephon "Starbury" Marbury was born in Brooklyn, New York, in 1977 and played for the Yellow Jackets from 1995 to 1996. In his only season with Tech, he averaged close to nineteen points per game and helped the team to a 24-12 record. He was the fourth overall selection of the 1996 draft by the Milwaukee Bucks. After several years and several teams he began a new basketball career in China.

Jim Nolan

Jim Nolan played basketball and football for Georgia Tech from 1946 to 1949. He was selected by the Philadelphia Warriors in the 1949 Basketball Association of America draft, but only played a few games in his professional career. He was inducted into the Georgia Sports Hall of Fame in 1962.

Mark Price

Mark Price was born in 1964, in Oklahoma. He played for Tech from 1982 to 1986 and was a two-time All-American. At Tech, he averaged close to seventeen points per game and dominated the free throw. In the NBA, he made 90 percent of his free throws and 40 percent of his three-pointers. He won the Three-Point Contest twice and was an All-Star four times.

John Salley

A native of Brooklyn, New York, John Salley was born in 1964 and began his college career at Tech in 1982. He averaged close to thirteen points and six rebounds per game while in college. Salley was the eleventh overall pick of the 1986 NBA draft by the Detroit Pistons. Recently, he has had a successful post-NBA career, appearing in movies, hosting *The Best Damn Sports Show Period*, and numerous reality television shows.

Dennis Scott

Dennis Scott was part of Tech's 1990 "Lethal Weapon 3" *(played by Joe Pesci)*. The small forward from Maryland was the 1990 ACC Player of the Year, averaging close to 28 points and 6.6 rebounds per game. In three years with Tech he averaged 21. 4 points, 1.5 steals, 2.9 assists, and 5.3 rebounds per game. He was the fourth overall pick in the 1990 NBA draft by the Orlando Magic and played with such teams as the Mavericks, Suns, Knicks, Timberwolves, and the Grizzlies.

Pete Silas

Pete Silas played for the Yellow Jackets from 1951 to 1953 and was All-SEC in 1953. He averaged 15 points per game and was one of the league's top rebounding forwards. In 1955, he played in the Pan-American Games and was also drafted professionally by the Minneapolis Lakers. Silas later became the CEO of Phillips Petroleum Company and was inducted into the Georgia Sports Hall of Fame in 1996.

Rich Yunkus

Rich Yunkus was the 6'9" forward who set Tech records while playing three years of varsity basketball. To start it off, he twice scored 47 points in a game. He averaged 24 points his sophomore year and his overall career average was 26.6 points per game. He holds the Tech record for most points in a career with 2,232. Matt Harpring is the closest competitor with 2,225 (he also played 40 more games). His number 40 is retired, and he was inducted into the Georgia Sports Hall of Fame in 1998.

Other Georgia Schools

Cindy Brogdon

Cindy Brogdon was the first Georgian to play basketball in the Summer Olympics, with the silver-winning 1976 US team. After playing a couple of seasons at Mercer, she transferred to the University of Tennessee. She averaged more than twenty points per game in her college career at Tennessee. Brogdon played professionally in a brief stint with the New Orleans Pride and in the All-Star game in 1980. She was inducted into the Georgia Sports Hall of Fame in 2002.

Anne Paradise Hansford

Anne Hansford was the first female from Georgia to be considered All-American, being selected three times. She played for the Atlanta Sports Arena Blues and the Chatham Blanketeers in North Carolina. She was inducted into the Georgia Sports Hall of Fame in 2003.

Sam Mitchell

Sam Mitchell was an exceptional basketball player for the Mercer Bears from 1981 to 1985. He set several records, one being the leader in points scored with close to 2000. Mitchell was the Atlantic Sun Conference Player of the Year in 1985, and was selected as the fifty-fourth pick in the 1985 NBA draft by the Houston Rockets. Later, he went on to coach for the Toronto Raptors for several years.

Pat Stephens

Pat Stephens was the star player for the Atlanta Athletic Club way back in the 1920s. He led the team to a record of 66-10 over six years. The team had winning records against Georgia and Georgia Tech, back when colleges and clubs would play against each other.

Amater Z. Traylor

Amater Traylor was an All-American basketball player from Atlanta. He played at Morehouse College and led them to a national championship in 1923. Later he became the secretary of the Georgia Interscholastic Athletic Conference throughout the time of integration in the 1960s. Traylor was inducted into the Georgia Sports Hall of Fame in 1988.

Roman Turman

Roman Turman was the first person to receive a full athletic ride to Clark College in Atlanta. He was an All-American in both football and basketball, averaging more than thirty points and twenty rebounds per game in his last year at Clark. Do I hear "Sweet Georgia Brown"? Yes, he played for five years with the Harlem Globetrotters in the late 1950s and briefly with the New York Knicks.

Professional Basketball

The story of the Atlanta Hawks began in 1946 when the Tri-City Blackhawks became one of the first teams in the NBA. After two seasons the team moved to Milwaukee. *Hey, just like the Braves.* Very good, Jimmy. You're learning... In 1955, the Hawks moved again, this time to St. Louis. One might say that the Hawks had their best years in St. Louis, entirely based on the fact that the franchise won its only championship there.

In 1968 Georgia received its first pro team. The Hawks franchise came to Atlanta with many thanks to Mayor Ivan Allen Jr. for his commitment to bringing professional sports to "the city too busy to hate." The new owners were former governor Carl Sanders and businessman Thomas Cousins.

The Hawks' first season was a great start for the team and the fans. They came in second place in their division with the help of Lou Hudson, Zelmo Beaty, Walt Hazzard (later Mahdi Abdul-Rahman), Joe Caldwell, and Bill Bridges. After beating the San Diego Rockets in the first round, they lost to the Lakers in the second round of the division finals. The second season in Atlanta took them to a first-place finish in the Western Division, but the Lakers ruled the court again in the second round.

The team made a rough adjustment to the Central Division and finished the 1970-1971 season with a 36-46 record. "Pistol" Pete Maravich was the Hawks' draft pick, and he made an easy transition to the NBA, averaging twenty-three points in his first season. The Hawks lost Hazzard to a trade and started on a downward spiral; eventually losing Hudson and Maravich to trades as well. In 1974, Maravich was dealt to New Orleans for several players who never amounted to anything, and Hudson was traded for Ollie Johnson (who was waived after a year). It was around this time that people began to wonder whether the team would last in Atlanta. The Hawks had the lowest attendance in the NBA for the 1976 and 1977 basketball seasons.

It was good news for the people of Atlanta when Ted Turner bought the Hawks in 1977. Adding players like Dan Roundfield and Tree Rollins, the Hawks began to turn things around in 1980. Coach Hubie Brown led the team to a 50-32, first place finish.

Unfortunately, they couldn't keep it up the following year, and Brown was fired with three games left in the season.

By being traded to the Jazz for Dominique Wilkins in 1982, All-Star John Drew would play a major part in making the Hawks one of the most exciting teams to watch in the 1980s. After a couple of average years under coach Kevin Loughery, the Hawks hired Mike Fratello to lead them to post season success. They lost in the first round of 1984 and didn't make the playoffs in 1985. The 1986 Hawks included the 5'7" Spud Webb (who won the slam dunk contest his rookie season), Glenn "Doc" Rivers, and Kevin Willis. This team of the late 1980s saw tremendous growth in game attendance and playoff contention.

The early 1990s saw that attendance drop off, as did the Hawks' performance. Lenny Wilkens, who was a star point guard for the St. Louis Hawks, was hired as the new coach in 1993. Then the unthinkable happened in the 1993-94 season: Dominique Wilkins was traded to the Los Angeles Clippers for Danny Manning. Talk about "changing horses mid-stream," this deal is thought to be one of the worst in Atlanta sports history.

The Hawks managed to pull off winning seasons throughout the late 1990s with Dikembe Mutombo, Stacey "Plastic Man" Augmon, Steve Smith, and Mookie Blaylock leading the way. For five consecutive years without Dominique Wilkins, they made the playoffs, but never past the second round.

The team hit rock bottom in 2000, even with the additions of Isaiah Rider and Jim Jackson. For eight straight seasons beginning in 2000, the playoffs were not on the radar, but it looked as though they were finally turning it around in 2008. The Hawks were shining a bit brighter with coach Mike Woodson hired in 2004, finally bringing the team into the post season with help from Josh Smith, Al Horford, and Joe Johnson. The Hawks made a post season trip for six years in a row (as of 2013). Hopefully in the future they can advance in the playoffs and perhaps win a championship.

Legends

Lou Hudson

Lou Hudson was born in Greensboro, North Carolina, in 1944. He was with the Hawks from the team's days in St. Louis. "Sweet Lou" played for the University of Minnesota and was drafted in the first round as the fourth pick by the St. Louis Hawks. In his senior year he actually played a game with a cast on his right hand and managed to score twenty points.

Hudson played eleven seasons as a Hawk and for several years he was part of the Hudson/Maravich duo that seemed unstoppable. On November 10, 1969, Hudson went 25 for 35 from the field and added seven free throws to tie a Hawks record of 57 points in a game. He was selected as an All-Star in 1969 and repeated this honor five more times in his 13 year career. At 6'5", "Super Lou" was not only a killer shot from the outside, but could pull down his share of rebounds, averaging five to six per game over several years.

After playing for two seasons with the Lakers, he retired in 1979. His number 23 has been retired by the Hawks and he is a member of the Atlanta Sports Hall of Fame.

PPG	APG	RPG	FREE%	Steals
20.2	2.7	4.4	.797	1.4

Pete Maravich

"Pistol" Pete Maravich was born in Aliquippa, Pennsylvania, on June 22, 1947. He is widely known for his remarkable career with LSU, where he averaged more than 44.2 points over three years. He set NCAA records for total points and points per game, and he was known for his 'globetrotter-like' moves. His former coach apparently watched all of his college tapes and stated that if the three-point line had existed at the time, Maravich would have averaged around 57 points per game. *Ridiculous!*

Pistol Pete was the third overall pick by the Hawks in the first round of the 1970 NBA draft. He signed a contract that would make people today drool and made the All-Rookie team. Even with Pistol Pete, the Hawks couldn't manage to make it past the first stages of the playoffs. Maravich was traded to the New Orleans Jazz after four years and two All-Star appearances as a Hawk.

Maravich's last season in the NBA was the same year the league adopted the three-point shot. He was 10 for 15 ...not a bad ending for the outside shooter. In 1988, he died of a heart attack while playing a pick-up game with friends.

After Maravich's passing, Gene Sapakoff of the *Post-Courier* wrote in 1988 that "the behind-the-back passes, the between-the-legs dribbling, the nonchalant 30-foot bombs, the blind assists, the mop of dark brown hair that danced with each head fake, the wilted socks...If Pete Maravich didn't invent modern athletic style, he and Joe Namath collaborated."

PPG	APG	RPG	FREE%	Steals	3 Pt%
24.2	5.4	4.2	.820	1.4	.667

Dikembe Mutombo

Dikembe Mutombo Mpolondo Mukamba Jean Jacque Wamutombo was born on June 25, 1966 in the Democratic Republic of Congo (formerly Zaire). He came to the United States on a scholarship to attend Georgetown University and set an NCAA record for 12 blocks in a game. With a height of 7'2", he recorded 8.6 rebounds and 3.7 blocks per game in his three years of college play.

He was an eight-time All-Star and was Defensive Player of the Year four times. His 3289 blocked shots are second on the career leader board and he averaged 9.8 points, 10.3 rebounds, and 2.8 blocks per game in his long career. After a blocked shot, he was known to wag his finger at the opposing player; later in his career this would earn him technical fouls. Oh yeah, his shoe size is 22. *No, No, No...*

PPG	APG	RPG	FG%	Blocks
9.8	1.0	10.3	.518	2.8

Tree Rollins

Is Tree his real name? No. *Didn't he bite someone?* Yes. Wayne Monte "Tree" Rollins was the 7'1" center for the Clemson Tigers in college and was drafted by the Hawks. He played with Atlanta from 1977 to 1988. Rollins is currently ranked tenth on the NBA's all-time blocks list, but when he retired he was fourth.

Rollins was no stranger to controversy. He was accused of getting paid or receiving gifts during his time at Clemson, but he has denied such accusations. On top of that, he was also known to throw an elbow or two, which led to all-out brawls. In one 1983 incident, he elbowed the Celtic's Danny Ainge, who ran up and tackled him in mid-court. As other teammates piled on, Rollins allegedly bit Ainge's finger. On another occasion, after exchanging words with Antoine Carr, Rollins filed a lawsuit claiming that Carr verbally and physically abused him and he threatened him with a razor. The suit was thrown out.

All of this aside, Rollins was one of the best centers in the game and his roots (pun intended) in the Hawks franchise will always be remembered in a positive light. Rollins has gone on to coach in the WNBA and the NBDL. *The D stands for developmental.* Thanks.

PPG	APG	RPG	FREE%	Blocks
5.4	.6	5.8	.700	2.2

Dan Roundfield

Dan Roundfield was born in Detroit, on May 26, 1953, and played high school basketball at Chadsey Senior. He was MAC Player of the Year in 1975 while playing for Central Michigan University and averaged 16.7 points and 13 rebounds per game in his college career. In 1975, he was the 28th pick by the Cavaliers in the NBA draft.

"Dr. Rounds" was an Atlanta Hawk for six seasons and was an All-Star for three of those years. He made the NBA All-Defensive First Team three times and the Second Team twice. His totals for the ABA and NBA are 14.3 points, 9.2 rebounds, and 1.4 blocks per game. Also, his .735 average at the free throw line is pretty impressive for a big guy. Unfortunately, he drowned while saving his wife in Aruba in 2012.

PPG	APG	RPG	FREE%	Blocks
14.3	2.0	9.2	.735	1.4

Spud Webb

Spud Webb's story could easily be a Saturday morning television special. At only 5'7", Webb could jump higher than thought humanly possible. Often scoffed at throughout his life by coaches, Spud Webb had to prove himself on in high school, college, and the NBA. When he got his chance with N.C. State, he averaged close to two steals and more than ten points a game. He was finally drafted by the Detroit Pistons after playing in an independent league, but was cut.

The Atlanta Hawks gave Webb the chance he needed in 1985, and from then on there was no more doubting. He averaged more than five assists per game in his career and almost ten points per game. Also, he played with the Hawks for six seasons and later for the Sacramento Kings, Minnesota Timberwolves, and the Orlando Magic.

It must be said that Spud Webb proved in 1986, to all who had doubted him that he was something special in 1986. He competed in the slam-dunk contest and beat his teammate, Dominique Wilkins, in the finals. He had two perfect scores, shocking Wilkins and the world.

PPG	APG	RPG	FREE%	Steals
9.9	5.3	2.1	.848	2.0

Dominique Wilkins

Dominique "Magnifique" Wilkins was the *best* Atlanta Hawks player in the history of the franchise. Wilkins was born in Paris, France (hence the name Dominique) on January 12, 1960. His abilities on the court redefined what is humanly possible. He made his start with the University of Georgia, where he averaged more than twenty-one points per game. After three years with UGA, he was the third draft pick in 1982 by the Utah Jazz, but was traded to Atlanta immediately.

In Atlanta, he dazzled fans with his moves and dunks and set franchise records in total points, field-goals, field-goal attempts, points per game, games, minutes, and steals (since broken). Besides these incredible feats, he ranks second in a number of categories like offensive rebounds. —*Who would've thought...*

His head-turning moves were put on display for the world to see in numerous slam-dunk contests. He won contests in 1985 and 1990, but was a close second in 1986 and 1988, earning him the nickname "the Human Highlight Film". Wilkins was an All-Star nine times and elected to the Basketball Hall of Fame in 2006. Fans living in Atlanta in 1993-94 will always remember the nauseating news that the Hawks traded Dominique for Danny Manning. *That's when Atlanta fans quit watching basketball and started drinking...*

PPG	APG	RPG	FREE%	Steals
24.8	2.5	6.7	.811	1.3

Kevin Willis

Kevin Willis was born on September 6, 1962, in Los Angeles, California, and played three years for Michigan State. He spent his first nine years in the NBA wearing number 42 as a Hawk. Willis averaged ten points, one block, and seven rebounds in his college career for the Spartans.

He was picked up by the Hawks in the 1984 NBA draft as the eleventh overall selection. The power forward/center was part of the Hawks team that included Dominique Wilkins, Spud Webb, and Doc Rivers. At 7'0"- he pulled down 11,901 rebounds and he averaged 12.1 points and 8.4 rebounds per game in his long career. There is also something to say about his longevity, considering he set an NBA record as the oldest player, at 45, to play in the NBA.

PPG	APG	RPG	FREE%	Blocks
12.1	.9	8.4	.713	.5

Notable Hawks

Shareef Abdur-Rahim

Born in Marietta, Georgia, in 1976, Abdur-Rahim played ball at Wheeler High School and later for the University of California, Berkeley. He played for the Grizzlies for five years before making his way back home to Atlanta in 2001. Shareef averaged eighteen points and close to eight rebounds in his 12-year career.

Stacey Augmon

Stacey "Plastic Man" Augmon played from 1991 to 1996 with the Hawks and was on the NBA All-Rookie First Team. In college at UNLV, he was voted First-Team All-American and was considered one of the best defensive players in the nation. He played for the United States in the 1988 Olympics, earning a bronze medal. In 2011, he became the assistant coach for the UNLV Rebels basketball team.

Zelmo Beaty

Zelmo Beaty was born on October 25, 1939, in Hillister, Texas, and luckily grew to be six foot nine inches. Beaty briefly played for Atlanta after the Hawks moved from St. Louis. He was an All-Star in 1966 and 1968 and had a career total of 15, 207 points (17.1 per game) and 9,665 rebounds (10.9 per game).

Walt Bellamy

Walt Bellamy was born July 24, 1939, in New Bern North Carolina. As a youngster, he played ball at Indiana University and set a school record of 1,088 rebounds in his career. He won a gold medal in the 1960 Olympics and was taken as the number-one draft pick in 1961. Bellamy played near the end of his professional career in Atlanta, from 1970 to 1974. He has a career total of 20,941 points (20.1 per game) and 14,241 rebounds (13.7 per game).

Mookie Blaylock

Blaylock took over the point guard position left by Doc Rivers in 1992. He played college ball at Oklahoma and was the twelfth overall pick in the 1989 NBA draft by the Nets. Mookie was known for his defensive abilities and was part of the NBA All-Defensive Team five times. He is the Hawks franchise leader in three-pointers and steals (1321).

Bill Bridges

Bill Bridges was born in New Mexico on April 4, 1939 and made his way to the University of Kansas to start a lifetime in basketball. He was 6'6" and mostly played power forward. All three of his All-Star appearances were with the Hawks. Bridges averaged 11.9 rebounds and 11.9 points per game throughout his thirteen-year career.

John Drew

John Drew was a 6'6" small forward who made his start at Gardner-Webb University in North Carolina. He played for the Hawks from 1975 to 1982 and was an All-Star in 1976 and 1980. Unfortunately, he was banned for life from the NBA for his ever-present addiction to cocaine.

Connie Hawkins

Although Connie "Hawk" Hawkins was only a Hawk for one year, he was an elite player who missed several years due to a gambling controversy. He was dunking in ways that people couldn't even imagine in the 1960s. He traveled across the United States as a Globetrotter and played in the ABL and the ABA before he was finally able to enter the NBA. When he did enter the league, he showed how a man can overcome ridiculous obstacles and make it to the top.

Al Horford

Alfred Joel Horford was born in the Dominican Republic on June 3, 1986. He played basketball as a center and power forward in college for the Florida Gators. He was an NBA All-Star in 2010 and 2011 and was the Haier Shooting Stars champion in 2011.

Joe Johnson

Former Razorback Joe Johnson was born in 1981, in Little Rock, Arkansas. He played for the Celtics and the Suns before coming to Atlanta in 2005. Johnson averaged more than twenty-one points in his seven years with the Hawks and was an All-Star for six of those seasons. He was traded to the Brooklyn Nets in 2012.

Jon Koncak

Jon Koncak was born May 17, 1963, in Cedar Rapids, Iowa. The Atlanta Hawks selected him with the fifth pick in the 1985 draft. He made this list due to his time with the Hawks and the fact that he signed a multi-million dollar contract that was higher than some of the best in the game, and Jonny was a reserve player. That is truly impressive, Mr. Koncak.

Moses Malone

Although Moses Malone only played a few seasons with the Hawks, he was an All-Star in his first season in Atlanta. In fact, he was an All-Star twelve times, not including twice in the ABA. His number has been retired from two teams; unfortunately Atlanta isn't one of them. He retired with a total of 29,580 points (20.6 points per game) and 17,834 rebounds (12.2 rebounds per game).

Bob Pettit

Bob Pettit never played a game in Atlanta, but he was a Hawk, and perhaps one of the best players in franchise history. He scored more than 20,000 points and 12,000 rebounds in his career. With eleven All-Star appearances in as many seasons, the power forward began and ended on a high note. He averaged more than twenty-six points and sixteen rebounds per game in his career, and led the Hawks to their only championship.

Doc Rivers

Glenn "Doc" Rivers is a Chicago native and played in college as a point guard for Marquette. After college, he was the thirty-first pick in the 1983 NBA draft by the Hawks and stayed with them for eight seasons. He averaged close to eleven points, two steals, and almost six assists per game in his career. After his playing days, he became a successful NBA coach for the Magic and the Celtics. Doc was Coach of the Year in 2000 and led the Celtics to a championship win in 2008.

Josh Smith

Josh Smith was born in and raised in College Park, Georgia, and was the seventeenth selection in the 2004 NBA draft. In 2013, "J-Smoove" has played nine seasons with the Hawks, averaging more than fifteen points, two blocks, and eight rebounds per game so far in his career. He has some records under his belt: as he is the youngest player to block ten shots in a game (19) and the youngest player to reach 1000 blocked shots (24).

Steve Smith

Steve Smith was born on March 31, 1969, in Highland Park, Michigan. The six-foot-nine-inch shooting guard played for the Hawks for five seasons and made the All-Star team in 1998. He received a gold medal for his part in the 2000 Summer Olympics. Smith set a Hawks single-game record with nine three-pointers

Jason Terry

The six-foot-two-inch guard spent five seasons with the Hawk,s from 1999 to 2004. He was a bright light in some of the darkest days in Hawks history. Terry is known for his range and is fourth on the career three-pointer record list, behind Ray Allen, Reggie Miller, and Jason Kidd.

Notable Georgians
Dale Ellis

Dale Ellis was born on August 10, 1960, in Marietta, Georgia. He was a two-time All American for the University of Tennessee and was drafted by the Mavericks as the ninth pick in 1983. A major threat from the outside, Ellis won the three-point shootout contest in 1989. After seventeen years in the NBA, he averaged more than fifteen points a game and shot 40percent from downtown.

Walt Frazier

Born in Atlanta on March 29, 1945, Walt Frazier attended the Howard School and played football, baseball, and basketball. After attending Southern Illinois University, he was the fifth overall pick by the New York Knicks in the 1967 draft. He was selected to the All-Rookie Team and became a seven-time All-Star. His jersey (10) was retired by the Knicks and he was inducted into the Hall of Fame in 1987.

Lloyd Free

Free's nickname growing up was "World" because of his mid-air abilities, and he legally changed his name in 1981 to World Bernard Free (World B. Free). He was born in 1953 in Atlanta and played high school basketball in Brooklyn. The "Prince of Mid-Air" played in the NBA for thirteen seasons and averaged over twenty points per game.

Dwight Howard

Dwight Howard was born in Atlanta in 1985 and dominated the court for Southwest Atlanta Christian Academy during high school. He chose not to attend college and was picked up in the 2004 NBA draft by the Magic as the first overall selection. Orlando desperately needed him and he met all expectations by scoring twelve points and bringing down ten rebounds a game. He spent eight years with the Magic before being traded to the Lakers in 2012. So far in his career, Howard is a two-time block champ, four-time rebound champ, and a seven-time All-Star.

Norm Nixon

Born in Macon, Georgia, on October 11, 1955, Norm Nixon went on to have his jersey retired by Duquesne University. The Lakers picked him as the twenty-second selection in the 1977 NBA draft and in 1978 he made the All-Rookie First Team. The two-time All Star averaged close to sixteen points and eight assists per game in his thirteen year career.

Elmore Smith

Elmore Smith was born in Macon, Georgia, in 1949, and grew to be seven feet tall. After playing college ball for Kentucky State, he was the third pick in the 1971 NBA draft by the Buffalo Braves. He averaged around twelve points, ten rebounds and almost three blocks per game in his eight-year career.

7

— Golf —

Way Back When...

A Pool Cue

Before the year 1895, there was no rule stating that a golfer could not use a pool cue to putt the ball in the hole. So if they had to make a rule to prevent it, then it must've been happening.

Use the Tee to Putt

According to the first rules of golf, set in Scotland, you must tee the ball up to a club's length of the hole.

Augusta National Club Rules (Home of the Masters) (which seem like they should be part of the 'Way Back When' section)

No Women

It only took until August 2012 for the Augusta National Club to admit its first female members: Condoleezza Rice and Darla Moore

Can I Join?

You can't apply; you have to be nominated by a current member.

My Beeper's Blowin' Up

No electronics allowed at the Masters. Period. (Cameras are okay during practice)

Antebellum

The first African-American was not admitted to the club until 1990.

History

As for the origins of golf, no one knows for sure. George Peper sums it up nicely:

> It might have been on a country road in Normandy, or in an alley near the Roman Forum. It might have been among sand dunes above the North Sea, or on a

hillside overlooking Peking. It might have been in a field in Flanders or a courtyard in London or on the frozen surface of a Dutch canal.

Many researchers suggest that an early version was played in Asia and made its way to Europe on the Silk Road.

Stick and ball games were being played all around Europe during the Renaissance, but the closest to golf seems to be the game of *colf* played by the Dutch, who played four holes over four thousand yards up until the eighteenth century. *Was that a par three course?*

It was 1744 when the first game was played with a set of rules —*as far as you know.* This game was in Leith, Scotland. The following were the original rules set forth by the Gentlemen Golfers of Leith and signed by John Rattray:

1. You must Tee your Ball within a Club's length of the Hole.

2. Your Tee must be upon the Ground.

3. You are not to change the Ball which you Strike off the Tee.

4. You are not to remove Stones, Bones or any Break Club, for the sake of playing your Ball, except upon the fair Green within a Club's length of your Ball.

5. If your Ball comes among water, or any watery filth, you are at liberty to take out your Ball & bringing it behind the hazard and Teeing it, you may play it with any Club and allow your Adversary a Stroke for so getting out your Ball.

6. If your Balls be found anywhere touching one another, You are to lift the first Ball, till you play the last.

7. At Holing, you are to play your Ball honestly for the Hole, and not to play upon your Adversary's Ball, not lying in your way to.

8. If you should lose your Ball, by its being taken up, or any other way, you are to go back to the Spot, where you struck last, & drop another Ball, And allow your adversary a Stroke for the misfortune.

9. No man at Holing his Ball, is to be allowed, to mark his way to the Hole with his Club, or anything else.

10. If a Ball be stopp'd by any Person, Horse, Dog or anything else, The Ball so stop'd must be play'd where it lies.

11. If you draw your Club in Order to Strike, & proceed so far in the Stroke as to be bringing down your Club; If then, your Club shall break, in any way, it is to be Accounted a Stroke.

12. He whose Ball lies farthest from the Hole is obliged to play first.

13. Neither Trench, Ditch or Dyke, made for the preservation of the Links, nor the Scholar's Holes, or the Soldier's Lines, Shall be accounted a Hazard; But the Ball is to be taken out and play'd with any Iron Club.

Over time, the game spread throughout the world, especially in the colonies of imperial Great Britain. America's oldest golfing club is in Georgia's most historic city, Savannah. Most historians agree that the club began, at the latest, in 1794. A notice in the *Georgia Gazette* in September 1796 calls for members of the golf club to attend a meeting to elect officers of the club for the coming year. By the end of the nineteenth century, golf was becoming a regular American pastime and there were well over one thousand golf clubs in the United States by the 1920s.

The Augusta National and the Masters

There are four major professional tournaments in golf: the US Open Championship, the British Open Championship, the PGA Championship, and the Masters Tournament. The Masters is the only tournament held in one place every year, the Augusta National Golf Club.

The club was founded by Bobby Jones and Clifford Roberts in 1934. They searched for the ideal place to design a course and found it on an old indigo plantation in Augusta, Georgia. They hired Alister MacKenzie to design the course and it has consistently been ranked by numerous organizations as one of the top golf courses in the world. It has gone through numerous changes since it was developed, including the addition of more than six hundred yards since the 1930s.

There are many traditions that go along with the Masters tournament. The one that everyone knows is the infamous green jacket. Since 1949, each Masters winner receives the jacket that members where at the club. Usually, the winner keeps it for a year and then returns it to the club. Previous year winners present the jackets to the new winners, except when it's the same winner consecutive years. If this is the case then it is presented by a club official.

There have been some famous and powerful members to the Augusta National Golf Club over the years. Some of the names are quite recognizable and include T. Boone Pickens, Robert Goodyear, Warren Buffett, Bill Gates, Tom Cousins, Carl Sanders, and Sam Nunn. There is no application process, just a nomination and a little luck and wealth.

Past Masters Champions

2013 Adam Scott
2012 Bubba Smith
2011 Charl Schwartzel
2010 Phil Michelson
2009 Angel Cabrera
2008 Trevor Immelman
2007 Zach Johnson
2006 Phil Mickelson
2005 Tiger Woods
2004 Phil Mickelson
2003 Mike Weir
2002 Tiger Woods
2001 Tiger Woods
2000 Vijay Singh
1999 Jose Maria Olazabal
1998 Mark O'Meara
1997 Tiger Woods
1996 Nick Faldo
1995 Ben Crenshaw
1994 Jose Maria Olazabal
1993 Bernhard Langer
1992 Fred Couples
1991 Ian Woosnam
1990 Nick Faldo
1989 Nick Faldo
1988 Sandy Lyle
1987 Larry Mize
1986 Jack Nicklaus
1985 Bernhard Langer
1984 Ben Crenshaw
1983 Seve Ballesteros
1982 Craig Stadler
1981 Tom Watson
1980 Seve Ballesteros

1979 Fuzzy Zoeller
1978 Gary Player
1977 Tom Watson
1976 Raymond Floyd
1975 Jack Nicklaus
1974 Gary Player
1973 Tommy Aaron
1972 Jack Nicklaus
1971 Charles Coody
1970 Billy Casper Jr.
1969 George Archer
1968 Bob Goalby
1967 Gay Brewer Jr.
1966 Jack Nicklaus
1965 Jack Nicklaus
1964 Arnold Palmer
1963 Jack Nicklaus
1962 Arnold Palmer
1961 Gary Player
1960 Arnold Palmer
1959 Art Wall Jr.
1958 Arnold Palmer
1957 Doug Ford
1956 Jack Burke Jr.
1955 Cary Middlecoff
1954 Sam Snead
1953 Ben Hogan
1952 Sam Snead
1951 Ben Hogan
1950 Jimmy Demaret
1949 Sam Snead
1948 Claude Harmon
1947 Jimmy Demaret
1946 Herman Keiser

1942 Byron Nelson
1941 Craig Wood
1940 Jimmy Demaret
1939 Ralph Guldahl
1938 Henry Picard

1937 Byron Nelson
1936 Horton Smith
1935 Gene Sarazen
1934 Horton Smith

Legends

Bobby Jones

Born March 17, 1902 in Atlanta, Bobby Jones accomplished so much in golf in such a small amount of time that -Bobby Jones = Golf. He once said that "the secret of golf is to turn three shots into two." One thing that sets him aside from the other golf greats was that he participated in tournaments before his age hit double digits.

His career has been divided into two sections, the lean years (from ages fourteen to twenty-one) and the fat years (from ages twenty-one to twenty eight). It was in the fat years that he accomplished his major wins. He left golf on a high note, winning the Grand Slam (the US Open, the British Open, the U.S. Amateur, and the British Amateur) at age twenty-eight. Jones is the only person to win these four championships in a single season. During his lean years, he was more like *Happy Gilmore* than anything else. Jones was known to throw his clubs and just quit in the middle of a game. Once he matured into the greatest golfer ever, he put all of the temper tantrums behind him.

He was also known for his intelligence too. He attended Emory Law School and practiced law after retirement from golf. Jones also helped develop one of the most amazing golf clubs in the world, the Augusta National Golf Club. The Masters tournament has been held there since 1934. What's even more unbelievable is that he was an amateur golfer and never earned any money for the tournaments he won. He was inducted to the Georgia Sports Hall of Fame in 1963 and passed away in 1971 after a long battle with a rare spinal disease.

Tommy Aaron

Tommy Aaron was not Hank's brother but did have a heck of a swing. He was born in Gainesville, Georgia on February 22, 1937. He started playing golf before he was a teenager and played in high school and at the University of Florida. It didn't take long before he joined the PGA tour in 1960, but wouldn't have his first big win until the Canadian Open in 1969.

Aaron finally hit the big time with the 1973 Masters win. This was truly the highlight of his career, a feat that he would not be able to top. He joined the Senior Tour in 1987 and five years later won the Kaanapali Classic in Hawaii. He was the oldest player to make the Masters Tournament cut in 2000.

Andy Bean

When describing Andy Bean, Barry McDermott from *Sports Illustrated* put it eloquently: "Andy Bean likes to fish. He also likes to hunt, wrestle alligators, bite covers off golf balls, drive cars like Burt Reynolds, have a good laugh, collect guns, argue with fools and 'wimmen' and play golf like a son of a gun."

He was born in LaFayette, Georgia, in 1953 and was an All-American three times at the University of Florida.

When he turned pro, Bean tallied eleven PGA Tour wins, including wins at the Bay Hill Classic (by seven strokes), the Atlanta Classic, the Hawaiian Open and the Doral-Eastern Open three times. He played in 587 events and made 103 top ten finishes. On the Champions Tour he has forty-one top ten finishes and three tour wins.

Jim Dent

Jim Dent was born on May 9, 1939 in Augusta, Georgia. Growing up right next to the premier Augusta National Golf course foreshadowed what was to come, but the obstacles were great because Dent was African American. He was often in trouble at home for sneaking onto the famous course to look for golf balls, but his determination was greater than a spanking. After caddying at the Augusta National Golf Club and a brief stint in college, he dropped out and moved to Atlantic City to work on his golf game.

When Dent turned pro, he won the 1976, 1977, 1978 Florida PGA Championship and the 1983 Michelob-Chattanooga Gold Cup Classic. His drives were amazing, but it would take time for his short game to develop. After years of fine-tuning his game, he became a wizard on the Senior PGA Tour. From 1989 to 1998 he accumulated twelve Senior PGA Tour wins. He's made more than nine million dollars on the Champions Tour and 131 top-ten finishes.

Dot Kirby

Who says playing miniature golf can't lead to national championships? For Dorothy Kirby, who was born at West Point, Georgia, in 1920, this just happens to be the case. She won the Georgia State Women's Championship five times and the National Titleholders Championships twice. She was also known for coming in second place in too many championships to count. After competing in the National Women's Amateur Championship for thirteen years, she finally won in 1951 by one stroke. In 1974, Kirby became the first woman to be inducted into the Georgia Sports Hall of Fame. All of this and she never turned pro.

Davis Love III

Born in Charlotte, North Carolina, in 1964, Davis Love has made Georgia his home for many years. He grew up in a family where golf was a fixture; his father was a golf pro who taught and played in many championships. This is how DL3 learned to love the game. As a young phenom, he earned a scholarship to the University of North Carolina and became the ACC champion in 1984.

His first PGA tour victory came in 1987 and he would go on to win twenty as of 2012. Love won the PGA championship in 1997 by five strokes. Some of the tournaments Love has won include the MCI Heritage (four times), AT&T Pebble Beach National Pro-Am (twice), the International (twice), the Players Championship... just to name a few. His last tournament win came in 2008 at the Children's Miracle Network Classic.

Larry Mize

Larry Mize was born in Augusta, Georgia, in 1958 and has only won one major tournament in his career; it just happened to be in Augusta. His win at the Masters Tournament was extremely memorable. It was down to Mize and Greg Norman (who seemed to be cursed at the Masters) and Mize chipped a 140 foot birdie for the win.

Mize has ten professional wins under his belt. Including the 1983 Danny Thomas Memphis Classic, the 1993 Northern Telecom Open, the 1993 Buick Open, the 1988 Casio World Open, the 1989 and 1990 Dunlop Phoenix, and the Johnnie Walker World Golf Championship. He has one win on the Champions Tour with the one-stroke victory in the 2010 Montreal Championship.

Larry Nelson

Larry Nelson was born in Fort Payne, Alabama, in 1947 but grew up in Acworth, Georgia. He didn't play golf until his early twenties and within a year of his first stroke he was breaking seventy. He made the PGA tour at the age of twenty-seven and won the PGA Championship in 1981 and 1987. This golf natural also won the U.S. Open in 1983 by one stroke, with Tom Watson as the runner-up. Nelson has won forty professional events and has nineteen Champions Tour wins. Many consider him to be one of the most underrated golfers of all time. He was inducted into the World Golf Hall of Fame in 2006.

Doug Sanders

Doug Sanders, known as the "Peacock of the Fairways," was born in Cedartown, Georgia in 1933. He played for the University of Florida on an athletic scholarship and helped lead the school to win the SEC championship. A little while later, he played in the Canadian Open as an amateur and won the tournament.

After turning professional he won twenty events throughout his career, including the Western Open, the Coral Gables Open Invitational, the Hot Springs Open Invitational, the Eastern Open Invitational, the Jacksonville Open Invitational, and the Bahama Islands Open. Sanders placed second in the 1959 PGA Championship, the 1961 U.S. Open, and the 1966 and 1970 British Open. He was inducted into the Georgia Sports Hall of Fame in 1975.

Tim Simpson

Born in 1956 in Atlanta, Tim Simpson attended UGA and turned pro in 1976. He has nine professional wins and was the PGA Tour's Comeback Player of the Year in 1989. As for the major championships, he has two top-ten finishes, both in 1990. Simpson was inducted into the Georgia Sports and Georgia Golf Hall of Fame in 2004 and 2006 and currently plays on the Champions Tour.

Hollis Stacy

Hollis Stacy was born in Savannah, Georgia, in 1954, and attended Rollins College in Orlando, Florida. She turned professional in 1974 and won four major championships: the 1977, 1978, and 1984 U.S. Women's Open, and the 1983 Peter Jackson

Classic. Other professional wins include the Birmingham Classic, the Mayflower Classic, the CPC Women's International twice, and the S&H Golf Classic twice. Stacy was inducted into the World Golf Hall of Fame in 2012.

Louise Suggs

Louise Suggs was born in Atlanta in 1923 into a sporting family. Luckily, she grew up playing on one of the golf courses built by her father and found she had a knack for the sport. Suggs helped incorporate the LPGA and was later its president. An award was created in her honor. She won an impressive fifty-eight contests and eleven major championships in her long career. Coming as no surprise, she has been inducted into the World Golf Hall of Fame and the Georgia Sports Hall of Fame.

Bubba Watson

Bubba Watson was born on November 5, 1978, in Bagdad, Florida, but attended college at the University of Georgia. He is known for being a lefty and having one of the longest drives in professional golf. So far in his blossoming career he has six professional wins, four of them on the PGA Tour. In 2012, he won the Masters Tournament, with Louis Oosthuizen as the runner-up. Watson has been seen (set up by Oakley) in a hovercraft golf cart and the video has been viewed several million times as of 2013.

<u>8</u>

— Auto Racing —

History

One word can sum up the beginnings of car racing in Georgia: hooch. *(Uh do what?)* That's right —hooch, white lightning, firewater, ole red eye, bathtub gin, home brew, mountain dew, rotgut, John Barleycorn, grog, blind squeeze, ya mama, or whatever you want to call it. Illegal corn liquor is the root of NASCAR. *How do ya reckon that is?* Well, the story goes back a ways and the setting would be in the foothills of North Georgia and North Carolina.

In the days of prohibition, people still wanted to wet their whistles and when there is a demand there is always a supply. *What is this, ECON 101?* The problem with this scenario is that whether or not booze was legal or illegal, the government wanted to get its fair share of money in taxes and revenue. So in order for the producers of the mountain dew to get it to their markets, someone was needed to "run" the rotgut. Say hello to day-trippers or what we now call race-car drivers. The drivers were needed to outrun police and revenuers on mountain roads day or night. They needed skills behind the wheel, mechanics to sup up their coupes, and a daredevil persona that could only be found in a Georgia country boy.

As the coppers became better drivers and literally gave the trippers a run for their money, the latter had to do something about it. What happened was that these drivers started finding excellent mechanics to fix up their cars, so a mix between good driving and a heck of an engine would get the brew to its destination. Some of the devices these mechanics installed are straight out of that old Nintendo game, *Spy Hunter*, like smoke screens and oil slicks, minus the surface-to-air missiles.

A sure way the law could tell if a bootlegger was haulin' whiskey was when the car was waited down from all the booze. The drivers would fix this problem by installing giant coils or springs that held the back end up in the air when the car was empty but looked perfectly level when it was full.

This was a dangerous job and often ended in a jail sentence or even death. It wasn't unheard of that a car would flip and the hooch would ignite. The drivers had to overcome slick, red-clay roads, weight-shifting loads of liquid in the car, troopers with rifles, roadblocks, and the inevitable chase. With all those obstacles, it was no wonder that some of the earliest racers were moonshine delivery men. What seems more difficult: the obstacles of bootlegging or riding around an oval-shaped dirt track?

Professional Racing

A man by the name of Ray Parks started bankrolling drivers in the late 1930s. These drivers were his cousins, Roy Hall and Lloyd Seay, and perhaps due to their work as Moonshine trippers, they dominated the racing scene. In Florida, another driver named Bill France was a threat to be reckoned with in the sandy tracks of Daytona. There were organizations, like the National Stock Car Racing Association, that existed, but a new organized body was needed to unify the sport. France pulled together around a few dozen people, including Raymond Parks, for a meeting at the Streamline Hotel in 1947. After a series of meetings that followed, the National Association of Stock Car Auto Racing (NASCAR) was born. There were many men at these meetings, and there isn't a single face on the origin of NASCAR.

The Strictly Stock Series began in 1949 and has changed names throughout the years to the Grand National Series, the Winston Cup Series, and the Sprint Cup Series. Georgia boys dominated the series in its first year, with Red Byron (of Alabama but who raced early in Atlanta) becoming the champion (the car was owned by Raymond Parks). Another Atlanta boy, Tim Flock, was the champion in 1952 and 1955. The most recent Georgia winner of the series was Bill Elliott in his Thunderbird in 1988.

Legends

Bill Elliott

Awesome Bill Elliott from Dawsonville, Georgia, blazed through the NASCAR scene on February 29, 1976 at North Carolina Speedway. With an accent that accurately represents his hometown, his humility is surely a reflection of the "Southern gentleman" found in Georgia and all throughout the South.

He won what is now called the Sprint Cup Series (formerly the Winston Cup Series) in 1988. In his long career, he raced well over eight hundred times and has been voted the Most Popular Driver sixteen times. "Million Dollar Bill" won the Daytona 500 in 1985 and 1987, the year he also he set a NASCAR speed record by averaging more than 212 miles per hour during qualifying at Talladega. Elliott was inducted into the Motorsports Hall of Fame of America in 2007.

The Flock Family

The Flocks were a family of stock car racers of the 1940s and 1950s that included Bob, Tim, Fonty and their sister, Ethel Mobley. Bob once began a race and, as it turned out, the police came on the track after him because of his moonshine business. He rode through a fence and led them on a multi-mile chase. Another time, he flipped his car during a race and instead of quitting, he and some fans flipped his car back over and he continued the race.

Tim's antics included for several races a monkey sidekick named Jocko Flocko. Fonty broke his pelvis and crushed his chest, fought in World War II, and had two NASCAR wins. Ethel (who may have been named after the gasoline that her daddy used) was one of the first women to race in NASCAR events, and she often raced in events with only men. The "Flying Flocks" were a family made of moonshine, tires, engines and hall-of-fame status.

Roy Hall

Born in Dawsonville in 1920, Roy dominated early stock car racing with his pedal-to-the-metal style of driving. He was known to get his car on two wheels around curves and was even less a race car driver than a bootlegger. Hall did stints in prison and once robbed a bank, but that's what ballads are written about (Jim Croce wrote a song about him). His daredevil tactics on the raceways made him a fan favorite, and his outlaw ways caused him to race in disguise on a few occasions. He set a record for driving ninety-two miles per hour on the beach of Daytona in 1946.

Bud Lunsford

With 1,139 races won in his career, Bud Lunsford was one of the best drivers of the 1950s and 1960s. He was different from a lot of the other racers in that he wasn't a drinker or a moonshine runner.

Bud had more wins than any other dirt-track racer in history and built Lanier National Speedway in 1981.

Raymond Parks

Raymond Parks was the man behind the men behind the wheel. *Say what?* He grew up in Dawsonville running moonshine and even did some time for his outlaw ways. He later owned the cars that would have several first place finishes by drivers like Lloyd Seay, Roy Hall, Fonty Flock, and Red Byron. Parks was one of the founders of NASCAR and with the help of his brilliant mechanic, Red Vogt, success came in the associations first year. He was inducted into the Georgia Racing Hall of Fame in 2002 and is a nominee for the NASCAR Hall of Fame.

Lloyd Seay

Parker Lloyd Seay was another Dawsonville driver who started his career as a day tripper at the ripe age of thirteen and learned how to drive on the mountain roads in North Georgia. His style involved keeping his hands on the bottom of the steering wheel, so he could do a 180-degree turn without taking his hand off the wheel. Lightning Lloyd had his first win in 1938 and his last one in 1941. He won races in High Point, Daytona Beach, Atlanta, and Greensboro, just to name a few. He won his last race at Lakewood (he started in last place), but the next day he was shot and killed by his cousin over a dispute involving the purchase of sugar for their moonshine business.

Gober Sosebee

Gober Sosebee was an unbelievably fast driver from (who would've guessed it) Dawsonville, born on October 15, 1915. He set a speed record at Daytona in 1949 and had more than thirty top-ten finishes in the Grand National Series, with two wins. Although incredibly sad, it seems sort of fitting that the "Wild Injun" died at the age of eighty-one by flipping a tractor.

9

— Boxing —

Boxing, or pugilism as it was once known, has its origins before writing and depictions of it can be found on Sumerian relief carvings.

One may think that boxing would have had a vast following in the South considering the backcountry rough and tumble fighting in colonial times. The truth of the matter is that morality and tradition swept the South during the Great Awakening and left a citizenry who lifted their noses to such atrocities as bare-knuckle boxing. As boxing gripped the North, filling multiple columns in northern newspapers during the early and middle 1800s, its only mention in the South was to deplore it.

On November 4, 1858, the *Atlanta Weekly Intelligencer* printed the following about boxing:

> The demoralizing effects of such performances…cannot be too strongly depicted. If it were simply the mauling and pounding of these creatures for their own private gratification, it would be much less deplorable. But little difference would be made if they were all to get up a general saturnalia, and destroy each other. But it is the gambling which is encouraged on such occasions, the brutality that is cheered, and all the coarse and vicious passions of the young that are developed, which forms the great public evil.

As time went on, the public sentiment became less preachy and local Atlanta newspapers began reporting on prize-fights around the country. It was going to take a while before any large boxing matches occurred in Georgia.

The mood of the South may have finally started to accept fighting as part of human nature by the end of the 1800s. Bill Arp (Charles Smith) wrote an op-ed about boxing in the March 27, 1897, edition of the *Sunny South*, stating that he would like to see a prize-fight, albe-it secretly: "If 10,000 may fight in defense of their country, then one may fight in defense of his home or his property, or even his good name. But both are wrong according to the Savior's teaching, and if only those be saved who lived up to those teachings, then we are all lost."

Even by the early 1900s, the prize-fight was illegal, although it was starting to make a presence in Atlanta. The presenters would go to great lengths to avoid the word prize-fight from their events. In a report on a fight in Atlanta on October 16, 1908, it was written that "it was carefully explained that this was purely a scientific exhibition and not a prize-fight, and this was evidenced by the presence of Police Commissioner Van Dyke..."

By 1910, a bill was passed prohibiting prize fights in the state of Georgia. Of course, this didn't affect bouts done in secret, nor did it stop amateur boxing. Later, even motion pictures of prize fights were banned. Eventually, folks would come in record numbers to theaters around the state just to hear the bout of heavyweights. Theaters charged admission, received news of the match by telegraph and detailed every punch. As communities began to accept the inevitability of this brutal sport, it grew and grew.

Legends
D. T. Bell

D. T. Bell was a Macon, Georgia-native who found his best success in the late 1930s, winning the Golden Gloves Middleweight Championship in 1938 and 1939. He was a pilot in World War II and was killed flying a P-46 Thunderbolt. Bell was inducted into the Georgia Sports Hall of Fame in 1999.

Ezzard Charles

Although he was born in Lawrenceville, Georgia, in 1921, he grew up in Ohio and was known as the Cincinnati Cobra. His pro career began at the age of nineteen as a light heavyweight. After World War II Charles was in the heavyweight division and defeated Joe Louis to become the heavyweight champion of the world. He is a member of the International Boxing Hall of Fame

Theodore Flowers

Maybe it's a bit like the song "A Boy Named Sue." Theodore Flowers probably became such a great boxer by defending himself against bullies. "The Georgia Deacon" was the first African American middle-weight champion. He was born in Camilla,

Georgia in 1895, but grew up in Brunswick. In a time of staunch racism in the South, he was able to blur the color line and had fans of every race. His record included 115 wins and fourteen losses in the middleweight division. He became the middleweight champion of the world in 1926, but died in 1927 due to complications during surgery.

When he died, more than seven thousand people attended a public ceremony in his honor. As there was silence, his sister belted out "no more Tiger, no more Tiger…Hold the boat and let me go…I want to see him again."

Larry Holmes

Born in Cuthbert, Georgia, in 1949, Holmes turned pro at the age of twenty-four after a successful amateur career. He defeated Ken Norton in 1978 to become the WBC heavyweight champion. Holmes consistently defended his title, even against Muhammad Ali, who had come out of retirement in 1980. He eventually lost his title to Michael Spinks in 1985 and retired after a failed attempt at a rematch. The Easton Assassin came out of retirement to fight Mike Tyson in 1988, and again in 1992 to fight Evander Holyfield. He lost both fights. Out of his 66 wins (44 of which were knockouts), he won 48 in a row; one short of tying Rocky Marciano's record.

Evander Holyfield

"The Real Deal" Evander Holyfield was born on October 19, 1962, in Atmore, Alabama. Atlanta has taken Holyfield as its own, considering that he grew up in the Gate City. He trained for years as a kid and was a bronze medalist in the 1984 Olympics in Los Angeles. Holyfield was controversially disqualified for hitting his opponent after the referee told him to stop.

He turned professional after the Olympics and landed in the light-heavyweight division. Holyfield received $75,000 for his first fight, and slowly worked his way up the pay ladder. He earned more than $30 million in his rematch against Mike Tyson.

He worked for several years to reach the heavyweight class and in 1990 was ready. The Holyfield quickly defeated Buster Douglas, knocking him down in the third round, to become the heavyweight champion of the world. He lost his title to Riddick Bowe in 1992, his first professional loss. After regaining the title in a rematch decision against Bowe, he lost it again in 1994 to Michael Moorer.

Holyfield had health problems dealing with his heart, so he retired ...briefly. He took on the infamous Mike Tyson in 1996 and beat him silly in the eleventh round for a huge upset. The most notorious fight, however, was the rematch the following year. Probably out of frustration for being outmatched, Tyson bit Holyfield's ear not once, but twice during the fight. He was disqualified, fined $3 million, and had his boxing license revoked for a year.

Holyfield eventually took on Lennox Lewis twice, once for a draw, and the rematch went to Lewis. He won the WBC heavyweight title for a fourth time by beating John Ruiz in 2000. After losing to Ruiz in a rematch, Holyfield faced Chris Byrd but lost by decision after the twelfth round. He made a comeback and won a series of fights in 2006 and beyond. His career record is 44-10-2, and he is the only boxer to hold four heavyweight titles.

Sugar Ray Robinson

Jake Lamotta said, "I fought Sugar Ray so often, I almost got diabetes." He was the first *Sugar* in boxing, as others have taken the name in homage to Robinson. Born in Ailey, Georgia he became, what many consider the best pound-for-pound boxer ever. As an amateur he was 85-0, and after turning pro he racked up a career record of 173-19-6.

William Stribling

William "Young" Stribling had the looks of an angel— and the fists of a devil. He was born in Bainbridge, Georgia, in 1904, and became a pro at sixteen. He never fought a black boxer, but he won 221 fights. The "Knockout" was inducted into the Georgia Sports Hall of Fame in 1965.

Sidney Walker

Sidney "Beau Jack" Walker was a lightweight, *though no one called him that to his face.* He grew up in Augusta, shining shoes as an adolescent. Early on he fought in 'free-for-alls', in which several boxers fought in a ring and the last man standing was the winner. After receiving some training he climbed the ranks of the lightweight ladder, becoming the title holder in 1942. Walker would lose the title and win it back by fighting Bob Montgomery in 1943. It is said that Beau Jack boxed in 118 matches and won close to 90 fights.

10

— Tennis —

The origins of tennis are shrouded in mystery. No one knows for certain how or why many of the rules came into being. Why is zero called *love*? Why is the score kept in intervals of 15? Why are there two serves? Why do so many players grunt? Why the short shorts?

First, the most common belief in the origins of the game is that the name itself comes from the French word *tenez*, which goes back to the thirteenth century and could have been brought back from the Crusades. There is a city in Egypt called Tanis and the word *racquet* has its origin from the word *rahat* in Arabic. So could the game have come from the Fertile Crescent? Some believe that at least the type of ball best suited for the game had its origins in this far away land.

The earliest form of the game had no racquet, but the palm of the hand was used. Later, some sort of binding was wrapped around the hand to hit the ball. By the fourteenth century a racquet that looked more like a paddle with which a nun would whack a student seemed to be the method for hitting the ball. It wasn't until the sixteenth century that the more modern racquet was developed.

The first mention of tennis in America is from a document by Peter Stuyvesant, the Dutch Governor of New York. In this 1659 proclamation, he states that October 15 is a day of prayer and fasting. On that day he prohibited certain games that included tennis, ball-playing, hunting, fishing, dice, and others.

Legends

Danny Birchmore
Danny Birchmore was inducted into the Georgia Tennis Hall of Fame in 2011. As a Bulldog first, he was the first student to become an All-American in tennis. He has the highest winning percentage in doubles and is third in singles. In 1969, he beat Jimmy Connors in a clay court singles match in Louisville, Kentucky.

Mary Louise Fowler
Mary Louise Fowler was inducted into the Georgia Sports Hall of Fame in 1983. She won the Georgia Open doubles title from 1947 to

1952. She was consistently ranked by the Southern Lawn Tennis Association from 1937 to 1961 until cancer ended her playing career.

Bryan Grant

Bryan "Bitsy" Grant was born in Atlanta on Christmas Day in 1909. He was a member of the US Davis Cup team in the 1930s, and he made it as far as the quarterfinals in the 1936 and 1937 Wimbledon Championships. Grant was also the National Clay Court champion in 1930, 1934, and 1935.

Jaime Kaplan

A native of Macon, Georgia, Jaime Kaplan was inducted into the Georgia Sports Hall of Fame in 2005. Her best days were in the mid-to-late 1980s and she played at Wimbledon, the French Open, and the US Open.

Kelly Jones

Kelly Jones was born at Fort Gordon, Georgia on March 31, 1964. He was part of the U.S. Olympic team in 1984 in Los Angeles. He played in several Grand Slam tournaments in singles and doubles and retired in 1998.

Melanie Oudin

Born on September 23, 1991 in Marietta, Georgia, Oudin is a star tennis player in the world circuit. She won the Grand Slam mixed doubles in 2011 in the US Open with Jack Sock.

Frank Owens

Frank "Hop" Owens was a singles and doubles star at Georgia Tech and is a member of the school's Hall of Fame. He was inducted into the Georgia Sports Hall of Fame in 1979.

Lisa Spain Short

Lisa Spain Short was the first woman to attend UGA on a full tennis scholarship and was an All-American three times. She played in the US Open, Australian Open, Wimbledon, and the French Open. As players do, she retired from professional tennis in 1987 and now coaches at the Atlanta Athletic Club.

11

— Soccer —

Games involving the kicking of an object, usually an inflated animal bladder, have been around for hundreds if not thousands of years. The modern form goes back to 1848 when students at the University of Cambridge developed the game close to what is seen and played today. Rules included throwing the ball in and not running with it. The term soccer is derived from *association football*, which was used to distinguish itself from other forms of football, like rugby.

Soccer has yet to draw in the crowds in the United States it does in other parts of the world. The soccer ball could be seen as the olive branch of Latin America, whereas our olive branch in the United States is a shared bottle of bourbon, or maybe a baseball. Practically every US kid plays soccer at some point, but the game is not seasoned spectator sport.

Georgia's first real taste of soccer came when Emory University organized a team in 1958. Other colleges like the University of Georgia organized clubs by the 1970s. As with most of the other professional sports, Atlanta got a taste of professional soccer in 1967, with the start of the Atlanta Chiefs. They were owned by the Atlanta Braves and played in the newly developed National Professional Soccer League. It was obvious that the team wouldn't last long because it couldn't draw a crowd. The *Herald–Journal* reported, "Georgia's most successful professional sports team on the playing field has been retired due to lack of fans. The Chiefs reportedly have lost $1.5 million since 1967." The team lasted until 1973 under coach Phil Woosnam, who became league commissioner. The franchise opened its doors again in 1979 under the ownership of Ted Turner and the Chief name would live on again ...for three years.

In 1995 Atlanta started a new team called the Atlanta Ruckus. After a few years, it changed its name to the Silverbacks in honor of the Atlanta Zoo's beloved gorilla, Willie B. The Silverbacks gave fans an option to choose a new name, with the Silverbacks leading the poll. *Chiefs* was on the list but lost. The team took a hiatus for a couple of years in 2009, but has returned and is trying all the marketing tricks in the book to keep going.

A standout player from Georgia is Josh Wolff, who was born in Stone Mountain, and played soccer for the University of South Carolina. He played in the 2000 Summer Olympics and the 2002 World Cup. He played in the MLS for several years.

12

— Hockey —

Hockey's origins could go back to the Native Americans of North America, perhaps the Vikings and their game of *knattleikr*, maybe the game of *shinty* from Scotland or perhaps a combination of all these and more. *Knattleikr* is mentioned in the Icelandic sagas of the tenth and eleventh centuries and shows similarities to modern hockey. Players used sticks, contact was allowed, and there is mention of penalty boxes. Sounds just like today. It is debatable whether or not they played ice, but if was played in Greenland then it had to be, right?

Hockey in Geaawwgia? We ain't got no frozen ponds! With the loss of the Thrashers, it may take a long time for the NHL to make its way back to the Peach State. The history of professional hockey in Georgia goes back to the 1970s, just after the time that all the other pro sports made their way to Atlanta. Tom Cousins bought the franchise for $6 million and designated it 'the Atlanta Flames'. He chose this moniker out of respect to a city and its population, which went through hell when it was burned down by General William T. Sherman during the Civil War.

The Flames overcame a few losing seasons and regularly made the playoffs in the last half of their stay in Atlanta. They had a lifetime record of 268 wins, 260 losses, and 108 ties. Due to poor attendance and money going down the toilet, the Flames relocated to Calgary in 1980.

In 1992, a new team tunneled up from the depths of Atlanta's depleted hockey soul in the form of the Knights. They were part of the IHL and in the Tampa Bay Lightning farm system. Winning the Turner Cup in 1994, the Knights were bound to make Atlanta their home for many years to come. But two years later, the Knights left Atlanta and moved to Quebec, taking the name Rafales, which is, I believe, French for "bursts of air." *More like farts if ya ask me!*

With the construction of the Philips Arena and the destruction of the Omni, a new hockey team made its way into the hearts of Atlantonites, the Atlanta Thrashers. Fans picked the name after Georgia's state bird, the Brown Thrasher. It is also coincidental that early in Atlanta's development, a man by the name John Thrasher built homes for those in construction of the railroad in the 1840s. This small community was called Thrasherville.

Starting in 1998, the Thrashers lasted twelve seasons, with only three winning ones. The team's only playoff performance was swept away by the New York Rangers in 2006. The Atlanta Spirit Group had been continuously losing money and finally sold the team to True North Sports & Entertainment in May 2011. The franchise moved to Winnipeg, Manitoba, and took back the name of the city's old hockey team: the Jets.

Anyone who wants to see hockey around Atlanta must travel to Duluth and watch the Gwinnett Gladiators, a minor-league team affiliated with the Phoenix Coyotes (who used to be the old Winnipeg Jets ...and the New Winnipeg Jets were the Atlanta Thrashers. *Uh do what?)* The Gladiators have done fairly well and made it to the Kelly Cup in 2006, losing to the Alaska Aces in five games.

Highlights

- Manon Rheaume played her first professional regular-season game with the Knights in 1992. Female First!
- There were lots of fights.
- Chris Chelios is the only Thrashers' player inducted into the Hockey Hall of Fame.

Notable Flames Players

Dan Bouchard

Dan Bouchard was the Flames goalie for eight seasons starting in 1972 and went with the team to Calgary in 1980. After his career he made his way back to Atlanta where he coaches college hockey for Life University. He had more wins than losses in his career and a 3.26 GAA over sixteen years.

Guy Chouinard

One of the best forwards to ever play for the Flames, Guy "Gramps" Chouinard was the all-time leader in points and assists for the franchise. He averaged more than thirty-one goals in the last four years in Atlanta. After he retired, he found success in coaching minor league teams.

Bill Clement

Bill Clement spent five years with the Atlanta Flames and even played two seasons in Calgary before retiring in 1982. He was an All-Star center twice for Atlanta, in 1976 and 1978. He went on to become an analyst, actor, and public speaker. Before his career with Atlanta, he was part of the Philadelphia Flyers team that won two Stanley Cup championships.

Ken Houston

Ken Houston was drafted by the Flames in 1973 and stayed until the team moved. He averaged about twenty goals playing forward for Atlanta and was known to get into a brawl or two. This tough guy could have probably made a career in boxing as well.

Pat Quinn

Pat "the Big Irishman" Quinn played defense for the Flames from 1972 to 1977. He served as the team captain when he first signed with them. Quinn went on to coach for several NHL teams after his retirement.

Jacques Richard

The second pick in the 1972 NHL draft, Jacques Richard didn't quite live up to the expectations that surrounded him. His career was filled with injuries and alcohol, sometimes alcohol-related injuries. He was also caught trying to smuggle cocaine across the Canadian border and sentence to several years in jail. Sadly, he was killed in a car crash after attending his fiftieth birthday party in October 2002.

Notable Thrashers Players

Eric Boulton

Eric Boulton spent six years in Atlanta as a left wing. He didn't accomplish much in terms of goals or assists, but definitely had his share of penalty minutes. "Big Boulton" was known as an aggressive player and once broke another player's jaw with an elbow to the face; it was apparently completely unprovoked.

Ray Ferraro

Ray Ferraro was the veteran the nascent Thrashers needed. He only spent a few years with the organization but posted 147 points in Atlanta from 1999 to 2002. He played professionally for eighteen seasons and accumulated close to 900 points in that time. After his playing career, he got into radio broadcasting in Canada.

Dany Heatley

Dany Heatly got his start with the Thrashers in 2001 and won the Calder Memorial Trophy for rookie of the year. He scored 41 goals in his sophomore season and was destined to become an NHL star. Unfortunately, he crashed his Ferrari and his teammate, Dan Snyder, died from injuries. Subsequently, he asked to be traded and found success on other teams like the Senators, the Sharks, and the Wild.

Bobby Holik

Bobby Holik was another veteran that the Thrashers added to their repertoire in 2005. His career started in 1987, and he spent ten of those with the Devils before signing with Atlanta. He was named team captain in 2007 and scored ninety-six points with the Thrashers. Holik retired in 2009.

Marian Hossa

After playing several years for the Ottawa Senators, Marian Hossa was traded to the Thrashers for Dany Heatley. He played in Atlanta for three years and was the first player in team history to reach 100 points in a season. Not surprisingly, he also helped lead the team to its first division title. After three years in Atlanta he went on to play for the Penguins, the Red Wings, and the Black Hawks.

Ilya Kovalchuk

Ilya Kovalchuk could be considered the best player in Thrashers' history. In less than eight seasons in Atlanta, he scored 328 goals (averaging over forty a year). He was reportedly offered close to $100 million to stay with the Thrashers, but Kovalchuk rejected the deal and was traded to the Devils in 2009.

Vyacheslav Kozlov

Vyacheslav "Slava" Kozlov spent seven years with the Thrashers after playing ten years with the Red Wings. He was the recipient of the Dan Snyder Memorial Award for the 2006-07 season. He totaled 356 goals and 497 assists in his NHL career

Marc Savard

Marc Savard was only with the Thrashers for three years and didn't even play in every game. He did, however, set the single-season franchise record for assists with 69. After his days in Atlanta, he played for the Boston Bruins as an unbelievable set-up man. He received two concussions within less than a year, seemingly ending his playing career.

Dan Snyder

Dan Snyder was a center for the Thrashers and played in only forty-nine NHL games. He died from injuries sustained from a car crash in which he was the passenger in Dan Healy's Ferrari. The Thrashers (and now the Winnipeg Jets) give an annual award called the Dan Snyder Memorial Award to the season's best team player.

<u>13</u>

— The Olympics —

1996

The city of Atlanta was chosen in 1990 as the site of the 1996 Summer Olympics, with Athens and Toronto being the other major contenders. Costs for the games were close to $2 billion, and events were held in Atlanta and surrounding cities. The highlights of the Olympiad were plenty, and its legacy is seen in the monumental structures built for the events.

Highlights

- Muhammad Ali lit the Olympic cauldron
- Michael Johnson won the 200-meter and 400-meter relays, an Olympic first.
- Many thanks to Billy Payne and Andrew Young for work in getting the Olympics in Atlanta.
- It was the first Olympics to feature mountain biking, beach volleyball, and women's soccer.
- The mascot Izzy, or Whatizit, was a computer generated blue blob of weirdness.

Legacies

- Turner Field
- The Georgia Tech student apartments (Olympic Village)
- Centennial Olympic Park
- The Centennial Olympic Torch
- The World Athletes Monument

Georgia Olympians

Brent Abernathy

Born in Atlanta on September 23, 1977, Brent Abernathy won a gold medal for his part on the US baseball team in the 2000 Summer Olympics. He played in the majors for Toronto, Kansas City, Minnesota, and Tampa Bay.

Lucinda Adams

Lucinda Williams Adams was born in Bloomingdale, Georgia, on August 10, 1937. She attended Tennessee State University and is a member of their hall of fame. The "Lady Dancer" competed in 1956 Olympics in Melbourne, Australia, and 1960 Olympics in Rome, Italy; winning a gold in the latter for the 100 meter relay.

Paul Anderson

Anderson was born on October 17, 1932, in Toccoa, Georgia. He won the gold medal in weightlifting at the Olympic Games in Melbourne in 1956. The Toccoan muscle man set numerous world records and was in the Guinness Book of World Records. But his name was removed when the weight he lifted was never actually confirmed (10,000-pound backlift).

Tate Armstrong

Tate Armstrong was born in Moultrie, Georgia on October 5, 1955. He played basketball for Duke University and won a gold medal in the 1976 Summer Olympics in Montreal. Armstrong played for three years in the NBA for the Chicago Bulls.

Sean Burroughs

Sean Burroughs, the son of major league MVP Jeff Burroughs, was born in Atlanta on September 12, 1980. He was part of the gold-winning US baseball team in Sydney, Australia in 2000. He played major and minor league baseball for such organizations as the Padres, Devil Rays, Diamondbacks, and the Twins.

Alice Coachman

Born in Albany, Georgia on November 9, 1923, Alice Coachman was the first African-American woman to win a gold medal. This amazing accomplishment came in London at the 1948 Summer

Olympics in the high-jump competition. There's no telling what might have happened if the Olympics hadn't been cancelled in 1940 and 1944 because of World War II.

Isabelle Daniels

Isabelle Daniels was born on July 31, 1937, in Jakin, Georgia. She won the bronze medal in the 1956 Summer Olympics in the 4x100-meter relay. She went on to coach in high school and in 1990 was National Coach of the Year. She is an inductee of the Georgia Sports Hall of Fame.

Teresa Edwards

Another athlete from Jackie Robinson's hometown of Cairo, Georgia, Teresa Edwards was born in that small town in 1964. She won four gold medals in women's basketball in the 1984, 1988, 1996, and 2000 Summer Olympics. She was also a Georgia Bulldog and was inducted to the Women's Basketball Hall of Fame in 2010.

Adam Everett

Adam Everett is another Georgia boy that won a gold medal for baseball in the 2000 Summer Olympics. He was born in Austell, Georgia, on February 5, 1977 and played for such major league teams as the Astros, Twins, Tigers, and the Indians.

Debbie Ferguson

Although Debbie Ferguson was born in the Bahamas and competed for her birth country in the Summer Olympics, she is an honorary Georgian due to her attendance at the University of Georgia. She won a silver medal for the 4x100 meter relay in Atlanta and won gold in Sydney four years later.

William Fields

Born in Forsyth, Georgia in 1929, William Beauford Fields was a Navy crewman. He won a gold medal for rowing in the men's coxed eights competition in the 1952 Summer Olympics in Helsinki. He retired as a US Navy commander in 1977.

Dexter Fowler

Dexter Fowler was born in Atlanta in 1986. He won a bronze medal with the US baseball team, which beat Japan in the 2008 Summer

Olympics. He excels at base running and led the majors in triples in 2010. In most opinions, he has quite a career ahead of him.

Vincent Hancock

Vincent Hancock is a two-time Olympic gold medalist in the skeet competition. Born in Port Charlotte, Florida, in 1989, he now lives in Columbus, Georgia. He is a sergeant in the US Army and stationed at Fort Benning.

Cheryl Haworth

Cheryl Haworth is a Savannonite (a term no one uses for people from Savannah, Georgia). She was born on April 18, 1983, and became an Olympic bronze medalist. Haworth competed in the weightlifting competition in the 2000 Summer Olympics in Sydney. She was also the Pan Am Games champion in 1999 and the Goodwill Games champion in 2001.

Reese Hoffa

Reese Hoffa was born on October 8, 1977, in Evans, Georgia. He won the bronze medal for the shot put in the 2012 Olympics in London. He won the gold at the 2007 World Championships in Osaka and a gold medal at the 2006 World Indoor Championships in Moscow.

Martha Hudson

Born in Eastman, Georgia in 1939, Martha Hudson was a star athlete at Tennessee State University. In 1960, she took a trip to Rome, and, while she was there, she picked up a gold medal in the 4x100 meter relay at a small competition known as the Olympic Games.

Sada Jacobson

En Guard! Fencers love it when you say that. Sada Jacobson grew up in Dunwoody, Georgia and later studied law at the University of Michigan. She won two bronze medals and a silver in sabre competitions during the 2004 and 2008 Summer Olympics.

Roger Kingdom

"I like hurdles." Roger Kingdom achieved Olympic gold, not once, but twice for the 110 meter hurdles competition in 1984 and 1988. He was born in Vienna, Georgia (much like Austria) on August 26,

1962. The hurdler later became a track and field coach at a division II school in Pennsylvania.

David Larson

David Larson was born in Jesup, Georgia, on June 25, 1959. He excelled so much at the freestyle that he thought that maybe he'd swim on over to the Olympics in 1984 and win a gold medal in the 4x200-meter freestyle.

Chaunte Lowe

A California native who attended Georgia Tech and made Decatur her home, Chaunte Lowe is an American record-breaker. Although her Olympic best is sixth place, she has received gold, silver, and bronze medals in the World, World Indoor, and Pan American Junior championships.

Steve Lundquist

One of the youngest inductees of the Georgia Sports Hall of Fame, Steve "Lunk" Lundquist was an Olympic swimming champion at the 1984 games in Los Angeles. His stroke of choice is the breaststroke, for which he won a gold medal in the 100-meter. He set several world records during his active days and was the honorary Olympic flag bearer at the games in Atlanta in 1996.

Katrina McClain

Although born in Charleston, South Carolina, McClain was a star player for the University of Georgia's Lady Bulldogs. She still holds records for UGA that include points per game in a season (24.9), field goals in a season (310), and free throws in a season (176). Twice she won gold medals in the 1988 Olympics in Seoul and in 1996 in Atlanta. She has been inducted into the Women's Basketball Hall of Fame and the Naismith Memorial Basketball Hall of Fame.

Mildred McDaniel

Mildred McDaniel-Singleton was born on November 4, 1933 in Atlanta. She could jump over a person who was 5'9". In fact, she set a world record in 1956 for jumping 1.76 meters high. This feat won her the Olympic gold medal in Melbourne, Australia. In 1983, she found a home in the Georgia Sports Hall of Fame.

Edith McGuire

In the 1964 Olympics in Tokyo, Edith McGuire won a gold medal in the 200-meter race. She also won two silver medals in the 100 meter and 4x100-meter relay. She has been inducted into the Track and Field, the Georgia Sports, and the Tennessee Sports halls of fame.

Antonio McKay

Born on February 9, 1964, in Atlanta, Antonio McKaye had a stellar career in track and field at Georgia Tech. He won a gold medal in the 4x400-meter relay in both the 1984 and 1988 Olympics. He also won gold medals in the World and the World Indoor championships. In 20013, he was a track coach at a public high school in Atlanta.

Ralph Metcalfe

Born in Atlanta on May 30, 1910, Ralph Metcalfe participated in the Olympics in 1932 and 1936, winning a gold medal in 4x100-meter relay in 1932. In the 1936 Olympics in Berlin, Metcalf came in second behind Jesse Owens in the 100-meters. He later became a politician serving in the House of Representatives from 1971 to 1978.

Elana Meyers

What do Elana Meyers and Herschel Walker have in common? The bobsled. Considering the low amount of snow in Georgia, becoming an Olympic bobsledder is quite the achievement, especially when you grow up in Georgia. Meyers participated in the 2010 Winter Olympics and won a bronze medal in the two-woman bobsleigh.

DeLisha Milton-Jones

Born in Riceboro, Georgia, in 1974, DeLisha Milton-Jones played basketball for the University of Florida and was a First-Team All-American in 1997. She was a WNBA All-Star three times and a WNBA champion in 2001 and 2002. She won a gold medal in the 2000 and 2008 Olympics. When her playing days were through, she became the coach for the ABA's Los Angeles Stars men's basketball team.

Edwin Moses

Born in 1955 in Dayton, Ohio, Edwin Moses attended Morehouse College in Atlanta. He won gold medals in 1976 and 1984 in the 400-meter hurdles. His career was far from finished, because he also received a bronze medal in the 1988 Olympics in Seoul. Moses was inducted into the National Track and Field Hall of Fame in 1994

Adam Nelson

Adam Nelson was born on July 7, 1975, in Atlanta and attended the Lovett School. He competed in the Olympics in 2000, 2004 and 2008, winning three gold medals for the shot put competition.

Mel Pender

Melvin Pender Jr. was born on Halloween in 1937 in Atlanta. As an amateur, he won the gold medal in the 1968 Olympics in the 4x100 meter relay. As a soldier, he served in the U.S. military and coached track at West Point. He retired from the military with the rank of captain.

Dwight Phillips

A native of Decatur, Georgia, born in 1977, Dwight Phillips won a gold medal for the long jump in the 2004 Olympic Games in Athens. He has also won gold medals at the World Championships in 2003, 2005, 2009, and 2011.

Matthew Robinson

Another famous athlete from Cairo, Georgia, Matthew "Mack" Robinson was the older brother of Jackie Robinson. He attended college at the University of Oregon, where he excelled in track and field, and was later inducted into the Oregon Sports Hall of Fame. Showing his American pride, he won a silver medal in the men's 200-meter race at the 1936 Olympic Games in Berlin.

Courtney Shealy

Born in 1977 in Columbia, South Carolina, Courtney Shealy kicked off her career as a swimmer for the Georgia Bulldogs. She competed in the 2000 Olympic Games in Sydney, Australia, and won gold medals in the 4x100 meter freestyle and the 4x100 meter medley.

Eric Lee Shanteau

Eric Lee Shanteau was born in Snellville, Georgia on October 1, 1983, and went to college at Auburn University. He received gold medals in the World Championships and in the 4x100 meter medley in the 2012 Olympic Games. Not only has he battled in the

Olympics, but he has fought against cancer as well. Truly a Georgia hero.

Sheila Taormina

Sheila Taormina was the first Bulldog to win an Olympic gold medal for swimming. Not only is she an excellent swimmer, she has competed in the Olympics in two other events. She placed sixth in the 2000 triathlon event and later participated in the 2008 pentathlon. Amazingly, she is the first female to participate in three different Olympic sports.

Ashley Tappin

Tappin was born in Marietta, Georgia on December 18, 1974, and has three Olympic gold medals as a freestyle swimmer. Not only can she swim, but her looks aren't too shabby either; she dabbles in modeling.

Angelo Taylor

Angelo Taylor was born on December 29, 1978, in Albany, Georgia. He later attended Georgia Tech, where he won the NCAA hurdles title in 1998. Taylor won gold medals in the 400-meter hurdles in the 2000 and 2008 Olympic Games. Besides the Olympics, he earned gold medals in the 2007, 2009, and 2011 World Championships.

Gwen Torrence

Gwen Torrence was born in Decatur, Georgia, in 1965. After attending the University of Georgia, she competed in the 1992 and 1996 Olympics. She has won three gold medals, a silver medal, and a bronze medal.

Forrest Towns

Forrest Towns was born in Fitzgerald, Georgia on February 6, 1914. In 1936, he was the first person from the state to be named to an Olympic team. Towns was also the first Georgian to win a gold medal, which he did in the 110-meter hurdles in Berlin. Later he was track coach for UGA until his death in 1991.

Terence Trammell

Terrence Trammell was born in Atlanta on November 23, 1978. He has competed in the hurdles in the 2000 and 2004 Olympics. He has competed in the World Championships in Paris, Osaka, and Berlin, placing second each time.

Wyomia Tyus

Wyomia Tyus was born in 1945 in Griffin, Georgia, and attended Tennessee State University. She won gold medals in the 100-meter race in the 1964 and 1968 Olympics. She was inducted into the Georgia Sports Hall of Fame in 1976 and the International Women's Sports Hall of Fame in 1981.

14

— The Individual and Outdoorsmen —

Cycling

There are supposed to be sketches of a bicycle by one of Leonardo da Vinci's pupils from 1493, but the velocipede, patented by Baron Karl von Drais of Germany, was the first bicycle-like machine. It was created around 1818 and had no peddles, was made mostly of wood, and crashed quite often.

A new model was developed by Denis Johnson of Great Britain soon after Drais's model, and this bicycle was generally called a hobby-horse. Years after this, the high-wheeled or penny-farthing bike was developed in France. They were fast but very dangerous. It is at this time that those with the adventurous spirit took to the bicycle.

Finally, the more modern "safety bicycle" was created, and with the development of John Dunlop's inflatable tire, a bike ride was more popular than ever. It became so popular that bicycle racing was included in the first modern Olympic Games in 1896. Although it waned in popularity in North America as automobiles were being mass produced, a resurgence occurred in the 1960s, not having stopped since.

One of the greatest bicycle racers of all time is *Bobby Walthour* from Atlanta. Walthour was born in 1878 and started racing in the 1890s. He went from being a sprinter to a motor-pacer (following a fast motorcycle or automobile for the slip stream). This was an extremely dangerous endeavor with many fatal accidents. Walthour endured broken ribs, collarbones, wrists, arms, and a fingernail or two. According to the *Baltimore American* in 1901, in one instance during a race on Manhattan Beach, after 47 miles "the crank on the left side of his wheel broke off…The little Georgian made a circuit of the track riding with his right foot and dismounted to exchange his wheel for a perfect one. He only lost half a lap by this mishap—"

He earned the nickname "Unbeatable" when he wiped the floor with some of Europe's best riders. After some serious injuries, including a bad concussion when he wrecked his bike on the Spandau bicycle track in Berlin in 1907, he slowly faded from the sport.

Hunting and Shooting

Here are a few standouts from Georgia in hunting and shooting:

Punkin Flock

Vera "Punkin" Flock began her shooting career by hunting when she was a young teenager. She ended up with the qualities of Annie Oakley. Considered one of the best trap shooters, Flock had thirty Grand American trophies under her belt and was an All-American more times than any other woman. She was inducted into the Georgia Sports Hall of Fame in 1995

Frances Poole King Garlington

Born in 1905, in Atlanta, Frances Poole King Garlington began her training in 1941 and five years later she won her first contest at the 1946 Grand. The *Atlanta Journal* named her Female Athlete of the Year three times. She is an inductee of the Trapshooting Hall of Fame and the Georgia Sports Hall of Fame. Her husband Ed was no slouch and is also a member of the Georgia Trapshooting Hall of Fame.

Fred Missildine

Missildine wrote the book on trap and skeet shooting —literally. His lifetime average was 98.6-x-100 and he won thirty contests in his long career. He was inducted into the Georgia Sports Hall of Fame in 1975 and the Georgia Skeet Shooting Association Hall of Fame in 1990.

Fishing

Fishing goes as far back as the first human being in Georgia. Fishing began as way to add to the food supply, but there's more to it than just catching a meal. There's an art to fishing and the best out there compete in tournaments all over the state. There's sport fishing off the coast, bass fishing on the many lakes, fly fishing in the mountains, and even the phenomenon of noodling.

Georgia's many lakes include Oconee, Lanier, Sinclair, Hartwell, Seminole, and many more. One note worth mentioning is that every single lake in Georgia is man-made. There are numerous bass-fishing tournaments year-round on practically every major lake throughout the state.

Fly-fishing is another type of angling that involves a skill one develops over many years. Some of the best spots for this type of fishing can be found in the mountain streams in the north. A few of the best spots include Conasauga River in the Cohutta Wilderness, the Chattahoochee, the Chattooga, and Cooper Creek.

Another type of fishing is noodling, also called hillbilly handfishing. It involves sticking your hand in hole in somewhat shallow water. What is supposed to happen next is that there will be a huge catfish where your arm used to be. The sport can trace its heritage back to the early native inhabitants, but it has only recently become legal in Georgia.

Paddling

Whether for a restful float down a calm stream or an adrenaline-filled rush through a giant wave, the paddling experience has attracted millions of participants. Some people enjoy the lazy inner-tube trip with a cooler floating close behind. These types of rivers are found all over Georgia. Other than a few shoals, the Chattahoochee is a perfect example of a river for the "floater." *I thought floaters were something else!*

There are also rivers and bodies of water for the wildlife enthusiast. A prime example would be the Okefenokee Swamp. Paddling around this area of South Georgia is sure to bring sights that include alligators, deer, otters, snakes (*red on yella, kill a fella*), black bears, bobcats, turkey, big-foot, and more.

Other rivers are for the more adventurous of heart and maybe even those with a death wish. The Cartecay is a fine journey that boasts some thrilling whitewater. There are a couple of class 2 or class 3 rapids (depending on the water level). The Upper Chattahoochee (above Lake Lanier) is an excellent trip that hosts some fun whitewater. Then there is the best that Georgia has to offer:

The Chattooga

The Chattooga River is divided into four sections. The first two sections don't need to be mentioned …boring. Sections three and four have some of the best rapids in America. With names like Soc-em-Dog, 7-Foot Falls, Jawbone, and Corkscrew one should be ready for anything on this river. It came to fame because of the movie *Deliverance*, based on the book by James Dickey. It was a thriller filmed on the Chattooga and in the Tallulah Gorge. *I've heard 'squeal like a pig so much, the words have lost all meaning.* This river has it all, from family action trips to flirting with death in Woodall Shoals' keeper hydraulic.

Tallulah Gorge

The Tallulah looks like something from another planet. There's one rapid after another for approximately a mile and the six hundred steps to the put-in don't seem to deter the expert kayakers. Some of the rapids include Tanner's Launch (Boof) (IV), Oceana (V+) Gauntlet (IV+), Bridal Veil (V), Zoom Flume (III+), Tom's Brain Buster (IV+), and Twisted Sister (III+). This dam-controlled river wasn't having regular releases until 1993, when an outpouring of paddlers took advantage of the brilliant whitewater.

Backpacking

The mountains of North Georgia provide hundreds of miles of hiking trails that can lead to a waterfall, a mountain view, or to Maine. There are short trails and long ones for however long your escape from the city needs to be. Here are a few notable trails:

The Appalachian Trail

The 2,167-mile Appalachian Trail starts on Springer Mountain in North Georgia and ends on Mount Katahdin in Maine. *What if you start from Maine?* About seventy-eight miles in Georgia traverse the Blue Ridge Mountains and climb peaks that include Blood, Tray, and Slaughter mountains. Many hikers have made it through Georgia in less than five days.

The trail's completion is due to the naturalist Benton MacKaye, who popularized the idea. With the formation of the Appalachian Trail Club, the project was completed around 1937. Earl Shaffer is the considered the first person to hike the length of the trail in one continuous journey in 1948. He later wrote a book about his journey entitled *Walking with Spring*.

The Bartram Trail

William Bartram traveled through the southeast around the time of the American Revolution and collected details of the flora, fauna, and Native Americans of the area. The Bartram Trail was developed along his approximate route through Georgia, South Carolina, and North Carolina. Close to 40 miles of it are in Georgia, mostly near the Chattooga River before it climbs Rabun Bald and enters North Carolina.

The Benton MacKaye Trail

Another long distance trail that runs through Georgia, Tennessee, and North Carolina is the Benton MacKaye Trail. The BMT is close to 300 miles long and has its southern terminus in the same spot as the AT …Springer Mountain. One can hike the trail up to the Smokies and connect with the AT and make it a 500-mile loop trail.

Climbing

Climbing for sport goes back to September 28, 1289, when…just kidding, no one knows when it started… There are some climbs that have been documented from long ago, like when the Roman emperor Hadrian climbed the volcano, Mt. Etna, in Italy. Many years later, Sir Edmund Hillary and Tenzing Norgay were the first people to reach the summit of Mount Everest. Although there are no peaks of that size in Georgia, there are spectacular spots to climb. Some of the best locations in the state are Lost Wall, Mount Yonah, Tallulah Gorge, Rocktown, Boat Rock, Currahee Mountain, and Shaking Rock.

Lost Wall is near LaFayette and has a huge sandstone face, while Mount Yonah is near Cleveland and is where the Army Rangers train. Shaking Rock is south of Athens and can range from easy to expert. Rocktown is a perfect bouldering site in the Pigeon Mountain Preserve, and Currahee Mountain, near Toccoa, has a range of options.

15

— Venues —

Ponce de Leon Park

The area just east of modern Midtown Atlanta was once a place of rest and relaxation. A spring there supposedly had medicinal value (hence naming it after Ponce de Leon). The area was known as Ponce de Leon Springs and residents were hopping on the trolley to this hot spot as early as the 1860s. As it transformed into an amusement park in the late 1800s, it was known as the "Coney Island of Atlanta." It held a lake, a theater called the Casino, a merry-go-round, a Ferris wheel, concession stands, and about everything one wanted in a nineteenth-century amusement park.

The four-acre lake was filled in and a baseball field was built; along with bleachers for more than eight thousand people. It was here that the Atlanta Crackers and the Black Crackers played their home games. A fire destroyed the baseball park, but it was rebuilt to be fire-proof by Rell Jackson Spiller. This field was an extremely unique place for fans and ball players alike. It differed from most baseball parks at the time in that there was a giant magnolia tree in center field. Besides the tree, there was a hill of ivy as well, which was considered in-play.

Besides hosting the two Cracker teams, there were other events held at the park. Jack Dempsey had a fight here when he was forty-five years old (eight years since his last fight) to show that he "still had it." He lost...just kidding, he won. He beat the tar out of wrestler Clarence Luttrell. The fight was recorded and can probably be found online; it's worth watching.

In the early part of the twentieth century, college football and high school games, were played in the park on a number of occasions. After the building of Atlanta Fulton County Stadium, Ponce de Leon Park was demolished. The only thing that remains of the original park is the old magnolia tree, which still stands at the edge of a shopping center.

Fulton County Stadium

With a capacity of more than fifty thousand spectators, Atlanta's Fulton County Stadium was home to the Braves and the Falcons from 1965 to 1996. With the Braves not moving to Atlanta until the 1966 season, the Atlanta Crackers played in the newly built stadium. The stadium hit max capacity on opening day of the 1966 major-league season.

Atlanta Mayor Ivan Allen Jr. had been trying for years to get a professional sports team to the city, and the first step was to build a modern stadium. After trying to swing a deal to get the Kansas City Athletics, Hotlanta finally ended up with the Milwaukee Braves.

Major moments in the stadium include:

- April 8th, 1974: Hank Aaron career home run number 715, breaking Babe Ruth's record.
- August 18, 1965: -the Beatles' only performance in Atlanta. (My Mom was there!)
- October 25, 1995: the Braves win the World Series
- August 2, 1997: the stadium was demolished

Today, there is a parking lot where the stadium once stood. An outline of the old stadium is on the ground, as is a monument in the place where Hank Aaron's homerun landed.

Lakewood Speedway

Lakewood began in the early 1900s as a fairground, with a horse track and roller coaster. The first car race was in late July 1917, with Ralph DePalma crowned as the champion. The variety of races included motorcycles, modified racecars, Indy cars, horses and, eventually, stock car. The Dawsonville Triumvirate of Raymond Parks, Lloyd Seay, and Roy Hall dominated the stock car scene in the late thirties and early forties.

The Omni

Before Philips Arena, there was the Omni Coliseum, which was the home of the Atlanta Hawks, Atlanta Flames, and later, the Atlanta Knights. The Omni was built in 1972 and seated between fifteen thousand and sixteen thousand people. Besides sporting events, there were concerts by Elvis, Van Halen, Michael Jackson, the Rolling Stones, Madonna, and Bruce Springsteen. Many professional wrestling events and political conventions took place in this arena. Due to its low seating capacity, rust, and lack of luxury, the Omni was torn down to make room for Philips Arena. A fun fact: *omni* means "all" in Latin.

Turner Field

Turner Field was originally built for the Summer Olympics in 1996 and was known as Centennial Olympic Stadium. After the Olympics, it became known as Turner Field, the home stadium for the Atlanta Braves. Fulton County Stadium was demolished and became part of the parking lot. In its first home game, the Braves beat the Cubs on April 4, 1997.

It was built for more than $200 million and seats around fifty thousand people. Outside the stadium are statues of some of the Braves greatest players, including Phil Niekro, Warren Spahn, and Hank Aaron. Another unique feature of Turner Field is that $1 tickets are available, but one could spend close to $100 for the Hank Aaron seats, as well. A fun fact: Chipper Jones got the first hit at Turner Field.

The Georgia Dome

The Georgia Dome was built in 1992 in downtown Atlanta. It has hosted a plethora of concerts, Olympic Games, Super Bowls, and the NCAA Final Four. Not only is it the home stadium for the Atlanta Falcons, it is now the stadium for the Georgia State Panthers football team. It can seat around seventy thousand people and has more than 150 suites. The Dome is starting to fade a bit, and its dark interior isn't the best experience for Falcon's fans. In fact, land purchases are being made for a new stadium to be built very soon. It looks like the Georgia Dome's days are numbered. A fun fact: there are over 30,000 feet of lines for the soda dispensers.

Philips Arena

After the Omni Coliseum was demolished, no time was wasted in building a top-of-the-line multipurpose arena. Philips Arena cost around $220 million and was completed in 1999. It became the home of the Atlanta Hawks, Atlanta Thrashers, and "Grease" On Ice. *Say whaaaat?* Some of the events and concerts that have been held at Philips include WCW Monday Nitro, Widespread Panic New Years, WWF "Raw is War," Ringling Bros. and Barnum & Bailey Circus, WWF Royal Rumble, Lil Bow Wow, WWE Smackdown, Yanni, Bette Midler, Tony Hawk's Boom Boom HuckJam, WWE

Reunion Tour, Cirque du Soleil, ACDC, and WWE Raw Live Supershow. *Weird choice of events. What's with the wrestling?* A fun fact: The Arena was struck by a tornado in 2008.

Sanford Stadium

Sanford Stadium opened up in 1929 and over the years expanded from about 30,000 to 92,746 seats. It is one of the largest stadiums in the country and some of the 1996 Olympic events were held there. It is known for the hedges that surround the field, which were planted on October 12, 1929. The stadium was built using loans from UGA alumni and was named in honor of Steadman Vincent Sanford, who became the university president and a major proponent of the athletic program. The first game in the stadium was against Yale, and UGA won 15-0.

Bobby Dodd Stadium

The oldest field in the south, Grant Field was the Ramblin' Wreck's playing field since 1905. Grant Field was originally named the Flats, but renamed after Hugh Inman Grant, who died of appendicitis at the age of ten. He was the son of one of the wealthiest men in Atlanta, so his dad donated $15,000 so Tech could build a grand stand. John Grant would go on to donate another $50,000 over the years. In 1988, the stadium was renamed after legendary coach Bobby Dodd, but the field itself is still called Grant Field. Bobby Dodd Stadium has a seating capacity of fifty-five thousand people. A fun fact: from 1971 to 1994, the field used Astroturf instead of grass.

Lake Lanier

Built for reasons that include: electricity, flood control, and water supply, it was after the fact that one of Lake Lanier's main uses was for recreation. Boating, sailing, rowing, and fishing are just some of the activities that occur on the lake. In fact, the rowing competitions for the 1996 Summer Olympics were held on the northern end of Lanier. You could easily tell that it was Lanier, because of the red clay ring that surrounds the lake. Another activity the lake has to offer is car racing. *I don't get it...* When the lake was built, many items were buried under the water, and one of those items was Looper Speedway. When the water levels get low enough, you can see the cement grandstand.

Afterword

I apologize if any information in this book is incorrect. Through extensive research, I triple-checked as many facts as was possible. Still, there are bound to be errors. Feel free to email me with any corrections, as I will make a second edition in the near future, and will gladly change any incorrect information.

This has been a wonderful experience, writing and researching about the origins of recreation in this beautiful state. I'm a Georgian as far back as my family tree will go, and take great pride in presenting a positive light on the state in which I was born. Thanks for all of those who read the book and didn't throw it in their fire place.

— Bibliography —

Books

Ashe, Arthur. *A Hard Road to Glory: A History of the African-American Athlete 1619-1918*. New York, NY: Warner, 1988. Print.

Bartram, William. *Travels of William Bartram*. [New York]: Dover Publications, 1955. Print.

Caruso, Gary. *The Braves Encyclopedia*. Philadelphia: Temple UP, 1995. Print.

Culin, Stewart. *Games of the North American Indians*. Lincoln [etc.: University of Nebraska, 1992. Print.

Darnell, Tim. *The Crackers: Early Days of Atlanta Baseball*. Athens, GA: Hill Street, 2003. Print.

Davies, Richard O. *Sports in American Life: A History*. Malden, MA: Blackwell Pub., 2007. Print.

Farnsworth, James T. *Colonial Games, Pastimes and Diversions (for the Genteel and Commoner)*. New York: Universe, 2003. Print.

Gamble, Thomas. *Savannah Duels and Duelists*. Savannah: Review & Printing, 1923. Print.

Garrett, Franklin M. *Atlanta and Environs; a Chronicle of Its People and Events*. Athens: University of Georgia, 1969. Print.

Gipe, George. *The Great American Sports Book: A Casual but Voluminous Look at American Spectator Sports from the Civil War to the Present Time*. Garden City, NY: Doubleday, 1978. Print.

Goodman, Michael E. *The Story of the Atlanta Falcons*. Mankato, MN: Creative Education, 2010. Print.

Gorn, Elliott J., and Warren Jay Goldstein. *A Brief History of American Sports*. Urbana, Ill. [u.a.: Univ. of Illinois, 2004. Print.

Hall, Basil. *Travels in North America, in the Years 1827 and 1828*. New York: Arno, 1974. Print.

Henderson, Robert W. *Early American Sport: A Checklist of Books by American and Foreign Authors Published in America Prior to 1860, including Sporting Songs*. Rutherford: Fairleigh Dickinson UP, 1977. Print.

Hudson, Charles M. *The Southeastern Indians*. Knoxville: University of Tennessee, 1976. Print.

Jackson, Harvey H. *Sports and Recreation*. Chapel Hill: University of North Carolina, 2011. Print.

Janson, Charles William., and Carl Samuel Driver. *The Stranger in America, 1793-1806*. New York: Press of the Pioneers, 1935. Print.

Kraus, Richard. *Recreation and Leisure in Modern Society*. Glenview, Ill. [u.a.: Scott, Foresman and, 1984. Print.

LeBoutillier, Nate. *The Story of the Atlanta Hawks*. Mankato, MN: Creative Education, 2006. Print.

MacCambridge, Michael. *America's Game: The Epic Story of How Pro Football Captured a Nation*. New York: Random House, 2004. Print.

Macfarlan, Allan A., and Paulette Jumeau. Macfarlan. *Handbook of American Indian Games*. New York: Dover, 1985. Print.

Mark, Rebecca, and Robert C. Vaughan. *The South*. Westport, CT: Greenwood, 2004. Print.

Mooney, James. *The Cherokee Ball Play*. Washington: Judd & Detweiler, Printers, 1890. Print.

Mooney, James. *James Mooney's History, Myths, and Sacred Formulas of the Cherokees*. Asheville, NC: Historical Images, 1992. Print.

Naismith, James. *Basketball: Its Origin and Development*. Lincoln: University of Nebraska, 1996. Print.

Nelson, Jon. *A History of College Football in Georgia: Glory on the Gridiron*. Charleston, SC: History, 2012. Print.

Owen, David. *The Making of the Masters: Clifford Roberts, Augusta National, and Golf's Most Prestigious Tournament*. New York: Simon & Schuster, 1999. Print.

Palmer, Peter, Gary Gillette, Stuart Shea, and Rick Benner. *The ESPN Baseball Encyclopedia*. New York: Sterling Pub., 2007. Print.

Peper, George. *The Story of Golf*. New York, NY: TV, 1999. Print.

Peterson, Robert W. *Cages to Jumpshots: Pro Basketball's Early Years*. New York: Oxford UP, 1990. Print.

Phillips, Ulrich B. *American Negro Slavery*. Teddington: Echo Library, 2006. Print.

Rader, Benjamin G. *American Sports: From the Age of Folk Games to the Age of Spectators*. Englewood Cliffs, NJ: Prentice-Hall, 1983. Print.

Rader, Benjamin G. *Baseball: A History of America's Game*. Urbana: University of Illinois, 1992. Print.

Riess, Steven A. *Major Problems in American Sport History: Documents and Essays*. Boston: Houghton Mifflin, 1997. Print.

Sachare, Alex. *The Official NBA Basketball Encyclopedia*. New York: Villard, 1994. Print.

Smith, Loran. *The University of Georgia Football Vault: The Story of the Georgia Bulldogs, 1892-2007*. Atlanta, GA: Whitman Pub., 2007. Print.

Smith, Ronald A. *Sports and Freedom: The Rise of Big-time College Athletics*. New York: Oxford UP, 1988. Print.

Stephens, William. *A Journal of the Proceedings in Georgia- 1737*. Farmington Hills: Gale Ecco, 2010. Print.

Struna, Nancy L. *People of Prowess: Sport, Leisure, and Labor in Early Anglo-America*. Urbana: University of Illinois, 1996. Print.

Stump, Al. *Cobb: A Biography*. Chapel Hill, NC: Algonquin of Chapel Hill, 1996. Print.

Thompson, Neal. *Driving with the Devil: Southern Moonshine, Detroit Wheels, and the Birth of NASCAR*. New York: Crown, 2006. Print.

Walsh, Christopher J. *Where Football Is King: A History of the SEC*. Lanham, MD: Taylor Trade Pub., 2006. Print.

Whitman, Malcolm D. *Tennis: Origins and Mysteries*. Mineola, NY: Dover Publications, 2004. Print.

Wigginton, Eliot. *The Foxfire Book 2: Ghost Stories, Spring Wild Plant Foods, Spinning and Weaving, Midwifing, Burial Customs, Corn Shuckin's Wagon Making and More Affairs of Plain Living*. Garden City, NY: Doubleday, 1973. Print.

Wilkinson, Jack. *Georgia Tech Football Vault: The History of the Yellow Jackets*. Atlanta: Whitman LLC, 2008. Print.

Zirin, Dave. *A People's History of Sports in the United States: 250 Years of Politics, Protest, People, and Play*. New York: New, 2008. Print.

Newspaper Archives

Athens Daily Banner
Athens Weekly Banner
Atlanta Constitution
Atlanta Georgian
Atlanta Journal
Atlanta Journal-Constitution
Atlanta Weekly Intelligencer
Columbus Enquirer-Sun
Daily Atlanta Intelligencer
Federal Union
Georgia Bulldog Newspaper
Georgia Gazette
Harlan Daily Enterprise
Herald–Journal
Miami Daily News
Milwaukee Journal
New York Herald
New York Times
Newburgh Daily News
Pittsburgh Press
Post-Courier
Red and Black
Rome News-Tribune
St. Petersburg Times
Technique
Union Recorder
USA Today
Washington Post

Web Articles

Aschburner, Steve. "Not Just the Human Highlight Film." *Sports Illustrated.* N.p., 13 Feb. 2009. Web. <http://sportsillustrated.cnn.com/2009/writers/steve_aschburner/02/13/wilkins.dunk/>.

————--"Atlanta 1996." *Olympic.org*. N.p., 2013. Web. <www.olympic.org/atlanta-1996-summer-olympics>.

Bamberger, Michael. "Saving Grace." *SI Vault*. Sports Illustrated, 21 Apr. 1997. Web. 2013. <http://sportsillustrated.cnn.com/vault/article/magazine/MAG1009928/2/index.htm>.

Barlament, James. "Georgia Southern Football." *New Georgia Encyclopedia*. University of Georgia Press, 4 May. 2006. Web.

Bennett, Dashiell. "The 10 Craziest Rules At Augusta National Golf Club." *Business Insider*. N.p., 07 Apr. 2011. Web. <http://www.businessinsider.com/weird-rules-augusta-national-2011-4?op=1>.

Bowers, Matt. "John Heisman." *New Georgia Encyclopedia*. University of Georgia Press, 27 August. 2009. Web.

Bowers, Matt. "Evander Holyfield." *New Georgia Encyclopedia*. University of Georgia Press, 7 July. 2007. Web.

Bowers, Matt. "UGA Football." *New Georgia Encyclopedia*. University of Georgia Press, 20 May. 2005. Web.

————"Dawg Sports, a Georgia Bulldogs Community." *Dawg Sports*. N.p., n.d. Web. 2013. <http://www.dawgsports.com/2006/3/16/211222/437>.

————"Discover Biography." *Bio.com*. A&E Networks Television, n.d. Web. <http://www.biography.com/people>.
       (-For Biographical information on Georgia Athletes)

Elliott, Josh. "Walt Frazier, Debonair Knick." *SI Vault*. N.p., 16 Apr. 2001. Web. <http://sportsillustrated.cnn.com/vault/article/magazine/MAG1022268/index.htm>.

Ennis, Lisa. "Dot Kirby." *New Georgia Encyclopedia*. University of Georgia Press, 11 March. 2003. Web.

Ennis, Lisa. "Louise Suggs." *New Georgia Encyclopedia*. University of Georgia Press, 11 March. 2003. Web

Fenster, Kenneth R. "Cecil Travis." *New Georgia Encyclopedia*. University of Georgia Press, 2 Jan. 2007. Web.

Fenster, Kenneth R. "Spud Chandler." *New Georgia Encyclopedia*. University of Georgia Press, 7 July. 2005. Web.

Fimrite, Ron. "The Emperor Jones." *SI Vault*. Sports Illustrated, 11 Apr. 1994. Web. <http://sportsillustrated.cnn.com/vault/article/magazine/MAG1005077/2/index.htm>.

Fontaine, Theodore. *Born in Slavery: Slave Narratives from the Federal Writers Project, 1936-1938*, 356, Library of Congress, Washington, D.C.

Forman, Sean, and Justin Kubatko. "Sports-Reference.com - Sports Statistics and History."*Sports-Reference.com - Sports Statistics and History*. USA Today Sports Digital Properties, 2013. Web. 06 March 2013.

————-"Georgia Bulldogs Basketball History - UGA." *Georgia Bulldogs Basketball History - UGA*. USA Today Sports Digital Properties, n.d. Web. 03 June 2013. <http://www.sicemdawgs.com/basketball/bk_his.php>.

Gorn, Elliott J. ""Gouge and Bite, Pull Hair and Scratch" The Social Significance of Fighting in the Southern Backcountry." *American Historical Review* 90 (1985): n. pag. Print.

Griffith, Jon. "Sports in Shackles: The Athletic and Recreational Habits of Slaves on Southern Plantations." *Voces Novae* II.1 (2010): n. pag. Web.

Head, William P. "Tommy Aaron." *New Georgia Encyclopedia*. University of Georgia Press, 23 Sept. 2005. Web.

Head, William P. "Glenn 'Pop' Warner." *New Georgia Encyclopedia*. University of Georgia Press, 26 May. 2006. Web.

Hill, John Paul. "Luke Appling." *New Georgia Encyclopedia*. University of Georgia Press, 18 Nov. 2002. Web.

Hill, John Paul. "Beau Jack." *New Georgia Encyclopedia*. University of Georgia Press, 11 March. 2003. Web.

Hill, John Paul. "Johnny Mize." *New Georgia Encyclopedia*. University of Georgia Press, 1 April. 2009. Web.

Hinton, Ed. "Parks' Passion Fueled Early NASCAR." *ESPN NASCAR*. ESPN Internet Ventures, 21 June 2010. Web. 2013. <http://sports.espn.go.com/rpm/nascar/cup/columns/story?columnist=hinton_ed>.

————--"History.com." *History.com*. A&E Television Networks, 1996. Web. 03 May 2013. <http://www.history.com/>.

Holtz, Sean. "Baseball Almanac." *Baseball Almanac*. N.p., 2000. Web. 01 June 2013. <http://www.baseball-almanac.com/>.

Hutson, William. *Born in Slavery: Slave Narratives from the Federal Writers Project, 1936-1938*, Library of Congress, Washington, D.C.

Johnston, Alexander. "The American Game of Football." *Century Magazine* XII (1887): 888-98. Print.

————"Inductees - Inductees." *Trapshooting Hall of Fame*. N.p., n.d. Web. 2012. <http://www.traphof.org/Inductees.html>.

Kaplan, Jim. "Old Dog With New Tricks." *Luke Appling, the Braves' 75-year-old Minor League Batting*. Time Warner Company, 23 Aug. 1982. Web. 17 May 2013.

http://sportsillustrated.cnn.com/vault/article/magazine/MA
G1125797/index.htm

Kaye, Andrew M. "Tiger Flowers." *New Georgia Encyclopedia.*
University of Georgia Press, 8 May. 2003. Web.

Kaye, Andrew M. "Young Stribling." *New Georgia Encyclopedia.*
University of Georgia Press, 14 April. 2006. Web.

Kimbrough, Bobby. "My Dad Founded NASCAR – An Interview
With Little Red Vogt."*OneDirt.* Power Automedia, 06 Mar.
2012. Web. 2013.
<http://www.onedirt.com/features/interviews/my-dad-
founded-nascar-an-interview-with-little-red-vogt/>.

Kirkpatrick, Curry. "More Than Georgia's On His Mind." *SI Vault.*
Time Warner Company, 1981. Web. 23 March 2013.
<http://sportsillustrated.cnn.com/vault/article/magazine/M
AG1124725/3/index.htm>.

Laird, Neil. "History of the Rules of Golf." *History of the Rules of Golf.*
Scottish Golf History, 2007. Web.
<http://www.scottishgolfhistory.net/rules_of_golf.htm>.

MacMahon, Tim. "Spud Webb More than Dazzling dunks." *ESPN.*
ESPN Internet Ventures, 16 Jan. 2012. Web. 07 June 2013.
<http://espn.go.com/dallas/nba/story/_/page/dallasmlk/s
pud-webb-overcame-doubts-carve-successful-nba-career-was-
more-just-dunks>.

McDermott, Barry. "Hey, Look At Ol'andy Bean Right Up There In
The Big Time." *SI Vault.* Sports Illustrated, 19 Mar. 1979.
Web. 2013.
<http://sportsillustrated.cnn.com/vault/article/magazine/M
AG1094730/index.htm>.

Minter, A. Binford. "Hank Aaron." *New Georgia Encyclopedia.*
University of Georgia Press, 23 July. 2012. Web.

Minter, Rick. "Racin' Today » Georgia Is On The Rise Again In NASCAR." *Racin' Today.* N.p., 11 July 2011. Web. 2013. <http://www.racintoday.com/archives/28363>.

————"NBA.com, Official Site of the National Basketball Association." *NBA.com.* Turner Sports Digital, n.d. Web. 17 February 2013. <http://www.nba.com/>.

Newton, David. "Elliott's Old-school Style refreshing." *ESPN.* ESPN Internet Ventures, 21 Feb. 2012. Web. 2013. <http://espn.go.com/racing/nascar/cup/story/_/id/75972 84/nascar-bill-elliott-old-school-nascar-needs>.

————"NFL, CFL, College Football Statistics and History - Totalfootballstats.com." *NFL, CFL, College Football Statistics and History - Totalfootballstats.com.* Totalfootballstats.com, 2010. Web. 03 June 2013.

————"Noodling." *Georgia Outdoors Classic.* Georgia Public Broadcasting, n.d. Web. 04 June 2013. <http://www.gpb.org/georgia-outdoors-classic/noodling>.

Pierce, Dan. "NASCAR." *New Georgia Encyclopedia.* University of Georgia Press, 13 August. 2009. Web.

Pierce, Dan. "The Flock Family." *Encyclopedia of Alabama: Flock Family.* N.p., 2007. Web. 23 May 2013. <http://www.encyclopediaofalabama.org/face/Article.jsp?id =h-1049>.

————"Players." *PGATOUR.com.* PGA Tour, n.d. Web. 2013. <http://www.pgatour.com/>.
     (-For Biographical and Statistical information for Golfers)

Pope, Bobby. "Georgia Sports Hall of Fame." *Georgia Sports Hall of Fame.* N.p., n.d. Web. 2013. <http://www.gshf.org/>.
     (-For biographical information on inductees)

Reed, Brandon. "Remembering Lakewood Speedway." *Georgia Racing History.com.* N.p., 26 June 2009. Web. 2013. <http://georgiaracinghistory.com/2009/06/26/rememberin g-lakewood-speedway/2/>.

Reed, Brandon. "Telling the Stories of Georgia's Racing Heritage." *Georgia Racing History.com.* N.p., 24 Feb. 2012. Web. 2013. <http://georgiaracinghistory.com/2012/02/24/drivers-from-dawsonville-have-dominated-daytona/>.

Reed, Germaine. "Charles Herty." *New Georgia Encyclopedia.* University of Georgia Press, 30 Sept. 2005. Web

Reed, William F. "A Dark Night In Kentucky." *SI Vault.* N.p., 21 Feb. 1994. Web. <http://sportsillustrated.cnn.com/vault/article/magazine/M AG1004856/>.

————"Rise Up: History." Atlantafalcons.com, n.d. Web. 2013. <http://media.atlantafalcons.com/assets/History_Section.pd f>.

Scranage, David. "Tommy AARON." *Sporting Heroes.* N.p., n.d. Web. 2013. <http://www.sporting-heroes.net/golf/u-s-a/tommy-aaron-2781/brief-biography-of-tommy_a05930/>.

Schultz, Adam. "Nobis: The Man, the Legend." *The Falcoholic.* SB Nation, 02 June 2011. Web. 2013. <http://www.thefalcoholic.com/2011/6/2/2199891/nobis-the-man-the-legend>.

Schwartz, Larry. "Pete Maravich, 40, Dies of Heart Attack." *ESPN Classic.* ESPN Internet Ventures, 05 Jan. 1988. Web. <http://espn.go.com/classic/s/moment020105-maravich-dies.html>.

Singleton, Tom. *Born in Slavery: Slave Narratives from the Federal Writers Project, 1936-1938*, Library of Congress, Washington, D.C.

Sloope, Terry. "Rudy York." *New Georgia Encyclopedia.* University of Georgia Press, 28 July. 2005. Web.

Starrs, Chris. "Vince Dooley." *New Georgia Encyclopedia.* University of Georgia Press, 6 May. 2011. Web

Steptoe, Sonja. "A Big Hitter Finally Hits It Big." *SI Vault.* Sports Illustrated, 10 Dec. 1990. Web. 2013. <http://sportsillustrated.cnn.com/vault/article/magazine/MAG1136071/index.htm>.

———--"The New Georgia Encyclopedia." *The New Georgia Encyclopedia.* Georgia Humanities Council and the University of Georgia Press, 2012. Web. 13 April 2013. <http://www.georgiaencyclopedia.org/nge/Home.jsp>.
(-For biographical information on Georgia's athletes)

———-"The Official Home of Georgia Tech Athletics." *Georgia Tech Official Athletic Site.* CBSsports.com, 02 June 2013. Web. 03 June 2013. <http://www.ramblinwreck.com/>.
(-For biographical information on Georgia Tech's Athletes)

Toton, Sarah. "Vale of Amusements: Modernity, Technology, and Atlanta's Ponce De Leon Park, 1870–1920 | Southern Spaces." *Southern Spaces.* N.p., 15 Jan. 2008. Web. 2013. <http://southernspaces.org/2008/vale-amusements-modernity-technology-and-atlantas-ponce-de-leon-park-1870-1920>.

Turnbull, John. "Soccer." *New Georgia Encyclopedia.* University of Georgia Press, 23 July. 2012. Web

Van Hook, John. *Born in Slavery: Slave Narratives from the Federal Writers Project, 1936-1938*, Library of Congress, Washington, D.C.

"The bases are loaded, and I wish I was too."

-Skip Caray

Index

V

Van Brocklin, Norm   106
Van Note, Jeff   112
Vick, Michael   15, 119

W

Walden, Bobby   80
Walker, Herschel   65, 67, 74-75, 78-
   79, 84-85, 95
Walker, Sidney   170
Walthour, Bobby   193
Warner, Glenn Scobey 'Pop'   82, 91
Washington, Claudell   31
Watson, Bubba   162
Webb, Spud   141, 145-146
Werner, David   72
West, Ernest E.   87
Wheeler, Phillip   102
White, Jo Jo   57
White, Roddy   107, 113, 116-117
Wilhelm, Hoyt   30
Wilkins, Dominique   130-132, 141,
   145-146
Willis, Kevin   141, 146
Wilson, Big Jim   81
Wingo, Ivey   58
Winn, Captain Bill   105
Wohlers, Mark   52, 58
Wolff, Josh   176
Wood, Leonard   87
Woodruff, Kid   65, 81
Woodson, Mike   141
Woosnam, Phil   157, 175
Wyatt, Whitlow   58

Y

Yeates, Jeff   119
Yellow Jackets   87, 133
Yunkus, Rich   138

Z

Zambiasi, Ben   81
Zeier, Eric   68, 81

23136651R00126

Made in the USA
Charleston, SC
10 October 2013